THE SECRET LIFE OF FRANCE

The Secret Life of France

LUCY WADHAM

faber and faber

First published in 2009
by Faber and Faber Limited
Bloomsbury House
74–77 Great Russell Street
London WC1B 3DA

Typeset by Ian Bahrami
Printed in England by CPI Mackays, Chatham

A version of 'The End of the Secret Garden' (Chapter 12) appeared
in *Prospect Magazine* in its online edition of December 2007

A CIP record for this book
is available from the British Library

ISBN 978–0–571–23611–4

2 4 6 8 10 9 7 5 3

Contents

v

Contents

For L.E.L.

. . . Remember where we are,
In France, among a fickle wavering nation.

Shakespeare, *Henry VI Part I*

1 Proposal

Driving and Breakfast

I was nineteen the first time Laurent Lemoine asked me to marry him. We had met in London when I was seventeen, the Christmas before my parents moved to Australia. A year later, he went to Sydney on business and took them out for an expensive dinner. It was a strange, old-fangled move but it achieved the desired effect. My mother rang me in a state of high excitement.

'He's gorgeous and he's definitely taken a shine to you!'

My father, who finds it difficult to resist a man who picks up the bill, was no harder to win over.

Laurent was my eldest sister Florence's flatmate. One day a French psychoanalyst would suggest that marrying him had been a form of deferred incest. I assume she meant between Florence and me, Laurent acting as a kind of stand-in (though using criteria this loose makes my whole family either perpetrators or victims of incest).

Florence had moved to France years before to escape her four younger sisters, and it would not be long before two of them decided to follow her: my elder sister Irene and, a year later, myself. Florence had brought Laurent to London for an English Family Christmas and he had settled into the sofa and played charades and watched our histrionics, interspersed, of course, with Quality British Television, as if he had been born to it. The sheer drama of my very female family had dazzled this brother of three, and his decision to marry me had, he later told me, been inextricably linked to his feeling of well-being that Christmas.

Laurent's first proposal came half a year later, in the summer of 1984. I had come to the end of my first year at Oxford. The holidays had begun and I was signing on for unemployment benefit in London. My parents had moved to Sydney with our younger sister and precious only brother and I was still torn between a giddy sense of freedom and the vertigo of abandonment. In their absence I spent most holidays with my best friend, but she had recently become involved in an abusive relationship, which had turned me into a reluctant and unwelcome witness, so I was looking for a job and somewhere else to live until the autumn term began.

One evening, I went round to have dinner with two of my university friends. They were planning a train trip round Eastern Europe and their first stop would be Paris. They offered advice about places where I might find work. I knew that if the worst came to the worst, I could always go and live with my boyfriend in his parents' house in Romford, but I was hoping to avoid this; our two-month-old relationship was already floundering and I was having escape fantasies. We had had a row three days before because he had caught me looking out of the window while we were having sex.

Proposal

I spent the night with my two girlfriends, and the next morning, having nothing better to do, I went to Victoria Station with them to wave them off. At the time I hadn't identified my pathological reluctance to be left behind and, unaware of my motives, while they were waiting for their train, I cashed in my dole cheque and bought a ticket to Paris. I thought I would go for a week to stay with Florence and then come back and find work.

The three of us took the ferry to Calais and then sat on what felt like a ludicrously modern train to Paris, newly upholstered in orange and brown and festooned with noisy French children playing cards. When we arrived at the Gare du Nord, the sun was setting and the streets were still warm from the heat of the day. As we emerged from the station, the smell of desiccated dog shit wafted up from the pavements and the dizzying miasma of human urine hung in every dark corner. A few years later this would be a thing of the past, not because people had stopped pissing in dark corners or because they picked up their dog's excrement but because Jacques Chirac, the long-standing mayor of Paris, set up a proud drone army in fluorescent green overalls which daily sprayed the pavements with dirty water from the Seine, leaving a whole new olfactory imprint on the city.

My girlfriends caught the Metro to their youth hostel and I went in search of a call box. Florence was not in. I left a message on her answering machine, then I called the only other number I had in Paris, the number of Florence's old flat. Laurent, of course, answered.

'Allô?'

'Hello, Laurent. It's Lucy. Florence's sister.'

'Ah Luç-ie! How are you? Are you coming in Paris?'

(However good his English would become during our years together, he would always cling on to that quaint Gallicism: Welcome in Paris!)

'I *am* in Paris. I'm trying to get in touch with Fly but she's not answering her phone.'

'It's a long weekend. She's probably out of town. Why don't you come here? Where are you?'

Fifteen minutes later Laurent pulled up outside the Gare du Nord in his improbably small car, a navy-blue Fiat 500, leant across and opened the passenger door. I climbed in and he kissed me on both cheeks, or more accurately on each corner of my mouth. Then we sped off up into the cobbled streets of Montmartre to his flat.

The last time I had come to Paris, Laurent had taken me out to dinner, after cleverly informing my sister that he fancied me. We had sat in a cramped restaurant on the Ile de la Cité and he had spent most of the evening talking about his ex-girlfriend, Aurélie, who had just left him for somebody else. Laurent explained that out of the sack Aurélie had bored him but that in it, she was unsurpassable. I suppose that he was deliberately throwing down the sexual gauntlet but all this news did was terrify me, and cause lasting damage to my self-confidence. What he didn't mention at the time was that his erotic infatuation with Aurélie had driven him to spend most nights hammering on the door of her new lover's flat, just like a character from one of the many *Nouvelle Vague* films that Laurent would later encourage me to watch as part of my instruction in French culture and consciousness.

While Laurent made me a plate of spaghetti with Gruyère, I tried Florence again. She was back home and eager to see me. I ate the spaghetti and accepted his offer of a lift across town.

Driving in Paris, even before I passed my test, has always been a pleasurable experience for me. I have never had a problem with yielding to traffic coming from the right. It's just a matter of getting used to the possibility that at any moment a car might shoot out at you from the most insignificant side street, crash into you and then hold you responsible. This puzzling rule which has thwarted so many English motorists was, in fact, adopted by the International Automobile Convention in Paris in 1926, confirmed in Geneva in 1949 and then again in Vienna in 1968. Known in English as 'nearside priority', this diverting ritual, so deliciously contrary to common sense, is nowadays suited only to the Parisians. That evening Laurent's own approach to this rule consisted of gaily tooting his horn at each intersection, like Noddy on speed. It was his way of warning everyone that he had no intention of conceding priority. The multitudes of reasonable roundabouts, which have since sprung up all over France, testify to the sad demise of this idiosyncratic driving rule.

The other distinctive feature of the Parisian motoring experience is of course the Place de l'Etoile, a huge roundabout with Napoleon's Arc de Triomphe in the middle, involving thirteen avenues, each one holding right of way. The Etoile has been written of endlessly as a symbol of French chaos. There are in fact rules – rules that are redolent of the game 'chicken' – they're just not the kinds of rules that come easily to Anglo-Saxon drivers.

Being a pedestrian in Paris is not as pleasurable as being a driver. It was some time before I learnt that zebra crossings were rather like Bosnia's 'safe zones': places where, if you die, you may simply die with the knowledge that your killer was in the wrong. For years, both my sister Irene and I waged dangerous and fruitless personal campaigns to force drivers to let us cross, striking guilt into their hearts when they did not. Irene could be seen in her very smart, manicured suburb of Paris, standing on a pedestrian crossing and yelling out the most florid of English obscenities, learnt mostly from her youth in the stands of QPR. After many years, we both conceded that it was a pointless and shaming business. Pedestrians do not have the power in France; cars do. It's as simple as that. Cross at a zebra crossing that is not served by a red light and the driver will probably call you a *mal baisée* (literally, a person who is poorly or infrequently shagged).

When I come to London I am so thrilled by the deference shown towards pedestrians that I find myself walking back and forth over zebra crossings, just for the joy of watching the car come to a halt and seeing that benign, closed-mouth smile, accompanied by the understated nod of magnanimity the English driver likes to give to the pedestrian.

It was Laurent who taught me how to drive. In his mother's battered 2CV only two weeks after my arrival at the Gare du Nord. For in spite of all my resolutions, it only took him a week to get me into bed. Seven days after that drive across Paris, I had moved in with him for the summer, and seven days after that he had taken me to Normandy to meet his parents. There, his mother Madeleine, who had a reputation as a terrifying misogynist, welcomed me warmly. After Aurélie and her high-octane sexuality, I was an agreeable respite.

My first French family breakfast struck me as a peculiarly messy affair. There are never any plates at breakfast time in France, so the trick, in the absence of plates and with limited cutlery (there are no knives, just a spoon in the pot of jam for collective use), is to daub your toast in mid-air above the table. Then, even the most polished French person, including my future mother-in-law, will proceed to dunk the toast – butter, jam and all – into their bowl of hot chocolate. When, years later, I mustered the courage to ask her if this wasn't a little ill-mannered, she looked up at me, chocolate seeping down her patrician chin.

'Bien sûr que non! On peut tremper au petit déj.' *Of course not. You can dunk at breakfast time.*

Although I was only nineteen, Laurent was thirty and ready to settle down. In September, before it was time to go back to Oxford, he took me on holiday to the Amalfi coast and proposed to me over a plate of *spaghetti vongole*. I told him that I was too young and suggested that he ask me again in five years' time. Ten months later we were married and our first child was on the way.

The journey that began at Victoria Station more than twenty years ago has pulled me – often against my will – into the bosom of a culture so different from my own that even today, with four children born and raised in France, I still struggle against the embrace. When I moved to Paris to be with Laurent we made a pact that I would make an effort to adapt to life in Paris but if, after five years, I was still homesick we would move the family to London. That was more than twenty years ago, and although Laurent and I are no longer together, I am still here. What follows is an attempt, by reliving my perplexed discovery, rejection and ultimate acceptance of this country, to understand why that is.

2 The Secret Garden

Slap and Tickle, Guilt and Parking

Laurent's extraordinary adroitness in pursuing me was one of the most attractive things about him; his self-belief was utterly compelling. The experience of sexual surrender was new to me. Until then, I had only known English boys my own age, who were all infected by a certain erotic timorousness, which had made it necessary for me to be the pursuer. It was always I who had to make the first move. Even the Jewish boy from Kingston-upon-Thames, who had received the gift of mother-worship and was therefore considerably more sexually confident than most, had waited for me to kiss him. On that occasion, a combination of desire and exasperation had driven me to spit tea in his face. This had freed things up and we never looked back. But he was the exception. Most of the time, having sex with English boys had meant battling my way through their insecurities long before we got anywhere near mine.

One of the things I noticed that summer about Laurent and his male friends was that they were all totally unreconstructed by feminist ideology. It was as if the feminist revolution had never happened in France. I wondered if some of the sexual paralysis afflicting my English male contemporaries was brought on by post-feminist guilt, which only seemed to compound the puritan tendencies inherent in our culture. Two of the boys I had slept with had actually confessed to feeling uncomfortable in the missionary position, saying that it made them feel 'too dominant'.

It soon became clear that this was not the kind of complex my future husband suffered from. Early on in our relationship his hand had shot out while we were having sex and slapped me smartly across the face. Supine and submissive as I might have been, the gesture backfired and my desire went out like a light. Laurent wasn't put off, though. He merely observed that smacks were obviously not my thing and that I shouldn't feel bad about it. He admitted that he had probably done it out of habit (Aurélie, the sex goddess, had apparently appreciated a carefully timed slap in the face).

In retrospect, my poor husband's erotic universe must have shrunk somewhat when I came into his life. What is certain is that after we split up, seventeen years later, he went back to some of his former sexual habits. For even though Laurent could hardly be called a libertine by Parisian standards, the opportunities offered by Paris's bourgeoisie for a tasteful kind of sexual adventurousness are both varied and plentiful.

Although my personal experience of sex with French people is limited, I would venture to argue, in spite of the old myths peddled about the French lover, that the quality of each individual sexual encounter is no better or worse in France than in England. Good sex and bad sex can of course be found everywhere, and one person's ecstasy is another person's nightmare. What I do believe, however, is that there is a climate surrounding sex in France which lends itself to a more open enjoyment of the seductive game.

For that is what sex is to the French: a game – with all the artifice that the word implies. The contractual nature of gender relations, both in Britain and America – requiring of us that we behave like adults – makes the kind of games played by men and women in France seem childish by comparison. For French women, the playing of games – the most hackneyed of which is not returning your lover's call for at least three days – is a vital part of their romantic arsenal. Overhearing my French-born, teenage children discuss their amorous affairs with their friends, I was often struck by the mixture of candour and duplicity that seemed to dominate their relations with the opposite sex – those hitherto workaday creatures whom they had sat beside in the classroom and whom they had now to pretend to worship. It has taken a long time for me to reach the point where I no longer judge this kind of behaviour. Looking beyond the often tawdry games French people play in the name of *la séduction*, it has become clear to me that the driving force behind sex in France is quite simply the pursuit of pleasure. Not ecstasy, not oblivion, but pleasure.

When Laurent and I began to live together, long before we really knew each other, I became aware of a gulf between our world views that I knew must be cultural. Mostly, we differed in our susceptibility to guilt. Laurent seemed to be virtually free of it. I was surprised to discover in his company how infected I was by various kinds of guilt: sexual, moral and political. It is hard to find examples of this since they go back a long way and I have been reformatted over the years to fit better into the French way of life. But I can tell that I have changed because when I go back to England I have a subtle but persistent feeling of discomfort, a kind of constant moral pressure to think and say the right thing.

This subtle feeling is, I realise, simply the result of habit. I know that my English and American friends feel a certain discomfort at the moral chaos that reigns in France. They dislike the discourteous driving, the queue-jumping, the fare-dodging, while I have come to find the level of civic obedience required in Anglo-Saxon society faintly oppressive. In London, I don't reverse down a one-way street because I know that some well-meaning old lady will rap on the window and tell me that I am going in the wrong direction. This would never happen in Paris, where everyone is constantly breaking the law. Only if the law-breaker inconveniences you personally do you ever bother to launch into invective. If the offender is an old person – ideally old enough to have been an adult during the Nazi Occupation – a classic and powerful taunt is to call them a collaborator. I remember the first time I heard this insult: an old man in a beret who was racing along the cycle lane in Paris alarmed a young man who was standing on the pavement, about to cross.

'Collabo!' the young man shouted, for all to hear. The old man nearly fell off his bike at the sound of that ugly diminutive but regained enough poise to raise his middle finger, leaving us onlookers to speculate on whether or not this had been the gesture of a collaborator or a *résistant*.

I never think of jumping the queue in London, while in Paris I do it all the time. Why? Because everyone is doing it. France is filled with disobedient children all busily trying to jump the queue. There is no guilt about this except, of course, for that special brand of shame you feel when you get caught.

I have read my Graham Greene and had always thought of guilt as the special ecstasy of Catholics. Since living in a nation of lapsed Catholics, I've come to realise that this is a gross over-simplification. The Catholic Church has certainly learnt over the centuries to use the idea of sin to great effect, but in comparing Britain, or indeed America, to France – all similarly developed, post-Freudian societies, one culturally Protestant and one culturally Catholic – it has been my observation that the dead hand of guilt falls far more heavily on us Protestants.

If guilt is the inner struggle between the *I want* and the *I should*, or as Freud would have it, the effect of the struggle between the Ego and the Superego, then Catholicism is the domineering but indulgent *Mother* and Protestantism, the aloof and exacting *Father*. The legacy of Catholicism in France is, amongst other things, her powerful and interventionist state; what Anglo-Saxons refer to as 'the nanny state' and the French more affectionately call *l'Etat-providence* (the munificent state). Under such a system, citizens are children, perpetually clamouring *I want, I want*; alternately scolded and mollycoddled by the powers that be. In both British and American society, on the other hand, where the citizen is supposed to behave like a self-regulating adult, guilt becomes a natural and highly effective enforcer.

I remember my delight as I began to understand the particular relationship the French have with the law. I had accumulated a few parking tickets and had started hiding them in my sock drawer, a habit of avoidance that would take me at least twenty years to break. Laurent caught sight of them one evening when we were dressing for dinner.

'I'm going to pay them,' I said.

'What year are we?'

'What?'

'1986,' he mused. 'It's worth waiting.'

'What for?'

'The presidential elections. There's an amnesty for parking offences at each presidential election. Better to wait for the next one.'

As the years went by, this lawless atmosphere worked its magic on me and I began to behave like everyone else. I would abandon my car – battered from the general practice of 'nudge parking' – on zebra crossings, pavements, traffic islands, while I ran in to collect my children. The

Parisian authorities have never resorted to clamping – they prefer to tow, since immobilising a car in a bad place doesn't make sense to them – but in those days, towing hadn't yet caught on and so the tickets began to pile up and the letters from *Monsieur le Préfet* became more and more insistent. The amnesty* seemed a long way off when fate intervened in the form of B., an employee of the *Renseignements Généraux*, or RG, France's bizarre, tentacular secret police force.

B. was a short man with an outlandish moustache and a thick southern accent whom I met while working as a freelance researcher for the BBC. He would occasionally invite me out to lunch and ply me with useless, often misleading information and I would go home with my head full of colourful detail of no use whatever to my employers. It was B., for instance, who told me the preferred euphemism used by RG spooks to indicate that the subject of their memo was homosexual: 'He is partial to the English style of life.'

Long after it became clear to B. and me that we were quite useless to each other, we still occasionally met for lunch. He had stopped trying to impress me by showing me where he kept his Smith & Wesson (in a holster round his ankle) and plying me with Chivas Regal in his office at the Ministry of the Interior. Instead we would meet for long, usually duck-themed lunches near the rue des Saussaies and exchange stories. He would talk in fast,

* Nicolas Sarkozy was the first president to decide to break this tradition – which never became law.

unrelenting police speak – an elaborately formal meta-language spoken by cops and understood by criminals – about the endlessly fascinating rivalries within the French police, and I would tell him about what life was like outside the confines of a surveillance vehicle. Usually over coffee, he'd click his jewelled fingers at me and hold out his hand for my parking tickets, which he would roll up and put in the pocket of his leather jacket, never to be seen again.

Adultery and the Cult of Beauty

In our Anglo-Saxon culture, sex and love have become polarised through guilt. In such a context sex can only achieve purification through love. There has always been a tendency in Britain and America to see sex without love as dirty. In the minds of the French middle classes, sex, even where love is absent, is a source of pleasure to which every human being has an inalienable right. Whether a person chooses to exercise that right or not is another matter.

In France sex is viewed, at its most basic, as a legitimate source of pleasure and, at its most elaborate, as an art form, a means of sublimation. For the Parisian bourgeoisie – and it is they who set the tone in this still hierarchical society – good sex is the single most satisfactory method of raising oneself above the monotony of everyday life. For this reason alone, drugs and alcohol do not have the same hold here as they have in Britain. When sex is combined with love, the French believe that its mood-altering effects are only intensified.

The belief in this idea explains the comparative toler-ance towards adultery, which filters down through all of society from the urban bourgeoisie and is reflected in liter-ature, cinema and the media. The French, led by the Parisian middle classes, are brought up to believe that if you're lucky enough to find erotic satisfaction within your marriage, then so much the better, but if you can't then you're entitled, so long as you remain discreet, to seek your fix elsewhere. As I would soon discover, even my future mother-in-law held this belief.

Laurent's mother, Madeleine, was a handsome and for-midably intelligent woman from an aristocratic family. His father, Jérôme Lemoine, was one of the nine stun-ningly beautiful Lemoine children of the sixteenth arrondissement, widely known in bourgeois circles for their parties, their small talk and their skill at dancing. When Jérôme and Madeleine met, he was leading a wil-fully vapid life scraping through an architecture degree at the Ecole des Beaux Arts, while she – one of the first women to be accepted by the prestigious School of Politi-cal Science, Sciences Po – was sitting in the cafés and cel-lars of Saint-Germain-des-Prés, listening to Jean-Paul Sartre and Juliette Gréco.

After ten years of marriage and soul-searching philo-sophical enquiry Madeleine met a Hindu guru in Paris by the name of Sri Menon and became one of his first disci-ples. Every year she would go for a spiritual refill at his ashram in the Indian state of Kerala and, as she soon made clear to me, it was in this way that she was able to turn a blind eye to her husband's chronic philandering.

I first got wind of my father-in-law's mistress the summer Laurent and I were married. Madeleine had been
away in India for the usual six weeks in spring and
Laurent and I were up in Normandy for the first time
since her return in order to discuss plans for the wedding.
I noticed that the house seemed uncharacteristically clean
and the kitchen cupboards in almost obsessive-compulsive
order. My mother-in-law was an efficient woman but she
was no domestic goddess, and I knew that the rows and
rows of homemade marmalade in the larder could not
have been her doing. When one of the jars appeared on
the breakfast table, I studied the label. 'Iris', it read.
'Spring, 1985.' As it turned out, Iris's excellent marmalade
had been enjoyed year after year by Laurent, his father and
his brothers – even by Madeleine herself – without their
ever once alluding to the mysterious English woman who
had settled into that house for six weeks to make it.

Four years later Iris would fall ill with cancer, and I
watched my mother-in-law stand by in mute misery while
her angry, grief-stricken husband spent night after night at
the other woman's hospital bedside. On one occasion
only, Madeleine confessed her distress to me. We were sitting in the kitchen of their flat in the sixteenth arrondissement.

'Why don't you leave him?' I asked.

She smiled kindly at me.

'What for?'

'He's making you suffer.'

'He's suffering more than me.' She pulled herself together and stood up to prepare lunch for her husband, who came home every day without fail. 'Anyway,' she said bravely, 'we don't do divorce in this family.'

It was Madeleine's profound conviction – one held by much of Paris's bourgeoisie, even today – that passion and desire should be accommodated within a marriage. You navigate your way through these emotions, treating your spouse as carefully as you can in the process. But on no account do you leave them.

Iris, the marmalade mistress, died of cancer and was replaced a few years later by another, younger woman, who also happened to be English. My mother-in-law accepted this new woman into the shadows of her marriage and only once lost her temper. When she discovered that, during one of her absences in India, her husband had brought their grandchildren to the woman's house for tea, she had asked Laurent, as the eldest son, to take his father out to lunch and have a word with him. Laurent obliged his mother and found that he didn't have to say much; his father knew he had crossed the line and Laurent was pretty sure it would never happen again.

When I first arrived in the mid-eighties, I was particularly shocked by an advertisement for 1664 beer that was showing in French cinemas at the time. A beautiful mother is collecting her little boy from school. Shots of her waiting with the other mothers for her child to appear are interspersed with shots of her with her lover, whom she has just left in a hotel room. Cut into the image of her little boy running towards her with his arms open are images of a hand unbuttoning her silk shirt, her long hair released from its pins, her head thrown back in sexual rapture. Philippe, a friend in advertising, explained the message:

'If you're a woman who drinks this brand of beer you'll be powerful and enviable, not bound by convention. You'll be the Total Woman – mother, lover, wife. You'll have everything,' Philippe explained. 'That ad was the beginning of a movement which started to depict women as sexy, mysterious, multi-faceted creatures who were in control of their destinies. It was the end of the housewife and the beginning of the sexually liberated woman.'

Of course, this particular vision of sexual liberation was completely lost on me. Accompanying our Protestant vision of sex as dirty is the feminist idea that to depict a woman as a sexual object is to degrade her. Embedded in my friend's explanation is the French belief that it is possible to use sex to sell without degrading women. As a result French advertisers have never hesitated in using sex in their campaigns, often to the exclusion of all subtlety, humour or creativity.

It is hard for me to rekindle the intensity of the moral outrage I felt on discovering French attitudes towards infidelity. I do remember interrogating my new husband on the subject like an inquisitive child.

'But what would you do if I went and slept with someone else?'

'I'd hope you wouldn't be stupid enough to let me find out.'

'But wouldn't you want to know?'

'No.'

'Why not?'

'What is the point?'

'Knowing the truth.'

'The truth is overrated,' he said.

After I had been in Paris for a few years, one of Laurent's acquaintances invited me out to lunch. I had sat next to him at a dinner party and he had asked me if I would be interested in doing some translation work. He was an auctioneer and often needed catalogues translated into English. The following week he took me to Fouquet's (an expensive restaurant off the Champs-Elysées, later favoured by members of the Yakuza [Japanese Mafia], now reputed among the Parisian haute bourgeoisie as flashy and vulgar, and where the upstart president Sarkozy went to celebrate his election victory). Once seated in a secluded alcove upstairs, the auctioneer proceeded to flirt with me so openly that I began to wonder if it weren't some elaborate joke. As he had the self-seriousness of certain very short men, I thought this unlikely. Then, over coffee, he came to the point: would I like to be his mistress? I laughed out loud. He looked me dead in the eye, his pouting little mouth twitching with indignation.

'I do not make jokes about such matters.'

I turned red with embarrassment.

'You don't have to answer now,' he said. 'Think about it. We would meet once, maybe twice a week. I will spoil you. Make you feel desired.'

'Thank you but No.'

'Do you not find me attractive?'

I began to cast about the room for an escape. He had asked for an isolated table. There were no waiters in sight.

'It's not that,' I stammered. 'I just don't want to be unfaithful to my husband.'

There was a long pause. He coolly observed my embarrassment.

'You should be careful then.'

'What do you mean?'

'You shouldn't make yourself available as you do. You give off signals that you're *disponible* [available].'

'Well, I'm not *disponible*.'

During that dinner with Laurent, then, he had got the idea that I was available. I had not yet learnt that the kind of chummy, asexual openness with which British and American men and women behave towards each other could be easily misconstrued in France.

Because of the ubiquity of the seduction game, Parisian women tend to cultivate a certain detachment, often approaching haughtiness. They keep up their guard with men, letting it down by mathematical degree according to the level of their sexual interest.

I came home that evening smarting with righteous indignation.

'Can you believe it?'

'Of course,' Laurent said, calmly folding his paper.

'But it's disgusting. He's supposed to be a friend of yours.'

'Not really.'

'And he invited me to lunch right under your nose.'

'He was just trying it on. If he fails, he's lost nothing.'

'God, I hope I never see him again.'

I did, of course, see him again. When we next bumped into each other, he pretended to have difficulty placing me. He clicked his fingers.

'Of course! Laurent's wife. How are you?'

The unwritten rule that the pursuit of erotic pleasure is a basic human right applies in France to women as well as men. As a result, French men, unlike Italian men, are not haunted by the spectre of the cuckold. The word *cocu(e)* can be applied to men and women, and adultery is widely perceived as one of the principal components of marriage.

On the next occasion that a member of Laurent's entourage made a pass at me I was better prepared. But this time my reaction indicated a very slight erosion of my moral defences.

I was researching a story for an English glossy magazine about literary salons in France. Laurent had told me about some aristocrat who had a castle in Brittany where members of the intelligentsia gathered to eat, drink and be highbrow. I had already interviewed the host, Jean-Daniel, in his office in the eighth arrondissement and was due to spend the weekend at his château in order to write a long, colourful piece describing the characters, atmosphere and events of one of these salons. He suggested we catch the train together on Friday evening.

Jean-Daniel picked a first-class compartment that remained miraculously empty on an otherwise busy commuter train, and it was only afterwards that I wondered if he might have bribed the guard. I sat down by the window so that I could use the table to make notes. Instead of sitting in the seat opposite me, he sat down beside me. He was considerably less repulsive than the diminutive auctioneer and I began to chat nervously, while he stared at me. When he took my hand and began kissing my fingers, there was a moment of hesitation before I pulled my hand away.

For the rest of the journey I barricaded myself in with banter and the appropriate body language, but I had let my guard down and he knew it. I avoided him all weekend and as a result the article was flat and lifeless and never got published. When, in a Protestant bid for transparency, I recounted the episode to Laurent, he was highly amused and admitted to feeling aroused by the picture of me having my fingers kissed on a train.

There is a saying in France that everyone is entitled to his or her *jardin secret* (secret garden). This quaint phrase tends to be a euphemism for infidelity and conveys the innocuousness of the sin in France. Today, in spite of rumours of an invasion of Anglo-Saxon prurience, the mainstream press, generally speaking, still regards the sex lives of French politicians as below their interest. Only the growing numbers of celebrity magazines, modelling themselves on British and American tabloids, are prepared to violate France's stringent privacy laws and pay the fines. The broadsheets are still too cautious to brave the tradition of shameless interventionism from politicians who can and will have people removed from their posts or relegated to *placards* (cupboards) – the term used for the dead-end jobs created for employees who have displeased the authorities. Even Sarkozy, who aspires to Anglo-Saxon transparency when it comes to his private life, couldn't help having Alain Genestar sacked as editor-in-chief of *Paris Match* after the news magazine published a picture of his then wife, Cécilia, with her lover. Sarkozy's behaviour was widely viewed as the petulance of the runner-up, rather than the action of someone trying to preserve his reputation.

The relative tolerance to infidelity in France is reflected both in the media and in the extremely stringent libel and privacy laws. French newspapers never hound a public figure for acts of infidelity. For many Anglo-Saxon journalists this is further proof of French gutlessness and pusillanimity. I think it is more to do with the primacy of pleasure over duty.

Not long after I had arrived in Paris for good, Laurent took me to a dinner party. The conversation touched on the newly opened Musée d'Orsay, which some felt was a triumph and others a failure. Everyone, however, approved of the curatorship of the collection. Anne Pingeot, the president's mistress, had been a good choice. When I asked how they all knew that she was the president's mistress, no one bothered to answer. When I went on to ask why it wasn't in the papers, a journalist from the weekly news magazine *Le Nouvel Observateur* took umbrage.

'What for? It's not news. Why should it be in the papers? It's no one's business who the president chooses to sleep with . . .'

Listening to him talk, I got the distinct impression that the journalist considered himself less a reporter than an arbiter of taste. He was also a kind of vassal, the guardian of his Lord's privacy. I listened, agog, as they went on to discuss the president's 'secret' love-child, Mazarine. The journalist sat with a knowing expression on his face while another guest lamented Mitterrand's choice of a rather gloomy flat for his mistress and their child. Someone remarked on its redeeming view of the Seine.

'He's been going there every evening to help Mazarine with her homework. Apparently, she's a good student. He hopes to get her into *Normale*.'

Normale is the absurdly inappropriate abbreviation for the impossibly competitive Ecole Normale Supérieure. Every year thousands of French children, who have been groomed by ambitious parents – often since birth – apply for about forty places. (At every parent–teacher meeting I attended I could always spot the mother whose child was being groomed for one of these *Grandes Ecoles*. She'd sit up at the front and interject incessantly in a booming voice, with all the authority of someone convinced that her offspring was destined to run the country.)

As for Mazarine, the years of private coaching from one of the nation's most erudite presidents paid off in the end. She got into *Normale* ten years later, specialised in Spinoza and came out fourth in her year. Indeed, it was the year she got into *Normale* that Mitterrand decided it was time he and the world recognised his brilliant daughter, his two legitimate sons, Jean-Christophe and Gilbert, having been a bit of a disappointment. (The elder would make his name as a fraudster and arms dealer, while the younger would forever languish in his father's shadow as a small-time apparatchik of the Social-ist Party.) Dying slowly at the time of prostate cancer, the president gave his permission for his 'secret family' to be revealed to the world, and the whole saga was told in full-colour pictures in *Paris Match*. Mitterrand had insisted on the presence of all three of his women – wife, daughter and mistress – at his funeral. When it finally took place in January 1996, the papers extolled the 'dig-nity' of the wife, Danielle Mitterrand, in the presence of a woman with whom she had been sharing her husband for more than thirty years.

Much has been written in the Anglo-Saxon press about President Sarkozy's new style of governance and the appar-ently un-French way in which he dangles his private life in front of the media. It is true that the easy summoning of *Paris Match* into his life with Carla Bruni would suggest a new frankness, a willingness to offer up his *jardin secret* to public scrutiny. In the early days of his liaison with the former model the president held a press conference at the Elysée Palace in which he famously announced their decision 'not to lie' about their affair. This did indeed represent a break with presidential tradition, but there was a certain continuity in President Sarkozy's deep-seated conviction that when it came to exercising his libido, the public would always be on his side. In the same press conference the president, with an undeniably flirtatious swagger, thanked TV journalist Roselyne Febvre for her question on his *vie sentimentale* and pointed out that she would never have dared to quiz his predecessors on their love lives, even when it was a known fact that they were 'playing away'. Alluding to Mitterrand's double life, Sarkozy announced his desire to end the 'hypocrisy' of former presidents and live in the open. He then went on to urge the press to exercise taste and restraint in their reporting of his life, requesting not to be photographed first thing in the morning (or indeed in the evening). The coy and admiring way in which the female journalist received the president's recommendations offered a perfect vignette of both France's sexual politics and the independence of her media.

The *jardin secret* is a right to which, in theory at least, everyone has access; in practice, however, like many rights in France, it is one that not everyone is able to exercise. Whether or not you have a *jardin secret* often depends on the gifts that Nature has endowed you with. Nicolas

Sarkozy, who, like Napoleon, makes up in libido what he lacks in height, is the exception to this rule.

France, for all her obsession with equality, has never attempted to level the erotic playing field. Beauty still carries high status here and no apologies are made for this. Rather than try to change this harsh reality, men and women do what they can to accommodate it. Most women in France – and more and more men – regularly visit a beautician. You will find an *esthéticienne* (beauty technician) in even the most remote villages; often, I have noticed, alongside a poodle parlour called – bafflingly – 'Doggy Style'. In line with all the other *corps de métiers* in France, the person plucking your eyebrows or waxing your bikini line will be extremely well qualified, with four years of training, a diploma in *esthétisme* and a great deal of pseudo-scientific vocabulary to go with it.

For a French person, man or woman, there is nothing to be gained by lamenting the superficiality of appearances, for in this culture appearances are all-important. The French are not only obsessed with Beauty in all of its manifestations; it is a value in itself. Everyone – in their physical being, their dress, their lives, their work, their homes – aspires either to *La Beauté* or to *l'Elégance*, its more democratic twin. No one is ashamed of this love of Beauty. It is triumphed and trumpeted everywhere you look. You only have to spend about ten minutes in France's capital city to feel the truth of this: the grand vistas, the façades, the fountains, the cobbles, the bridges, the lighting, the shop windows, the signage, the awnings, the street furniture, even the men in fluorescent green who pick up your rubbish before it hits the ground, all conspire to achieve one thing – to keep everything looking beautiful. Paris is all about Beauty. Everything else – including such things as commercial gain, prosperity or efficiency – is secondary.

For the French, Beauty does not reside exclusively in the past. It is a living, breathing, endlessly mutating deity. They're not afraid of modernity, as long as it is beautiful: the TGV is fast but, above all, beautiful; the glass pyramid that was placed in the courtyard of the Palais du Louvre was 'highly contested at the time and yet so beautiful in its transparent purity', raves a tourist guide to Paris's monuments.

It is interesting to compare the aesthetic legacies of two adjacent presidents, Chirac and Mitterrand. Jacques Chirac's presidency was not wreathed in the same prestige of magnificent architectural *Grands Travaux* as Mitterrand's was, simply because he had bad taste. Chirac is associated with the monumentally ugly Palais des Congrès on the Porte Maillot, a Soviet-style edifice built while he was prime minister under Giscard d'Estaing. Caving in to pressure, Chirac tried to make this building right in the nineties by spending 500 million euros on having it refaced by one of Mitterrand's favourite architects, Christian de Porzemparc. When, as newly elected mayor of Paris, Chirac unilaterally chose Jean Willerval's steel and chrome 'umbrellas' for the site of Paris's old food market (Forum des Halles), it became clear that he could not be trusted, and he was strongly discouraged from attempting to impose his architectural taste on the city again.

As an English woman I am still unsettled by the French obsession for physical beauty. My Protestant mistrust for the cult of appearances is deeply entrenched, and I find myself wincing when my own daughter excitedly tells me about a brand-new friendship: 'She's great. We talked all through lunch. She's so sharp and funny and she's really beautiful. She has the whitest skin and very dark eyes and these lovely long fingers which she uses all the time when she speaks . . .'

I have to remind myself that what my daughter is expressing is her deep cultural encoding for the myriad manifestations of Beauty. In some ways I find it touching that she is so affected by another girl's beauty and then I fear that she, like all her girlfriends, experiences levels of insecurity about her appearance from which I, in my own culture, was shielded. But then I remind myself that there is no equivalent in France to the sheer power of Anglo-Saxon-style magazines, and while political correctness may seek to preserve young women from physical stereotyping, British and American celebrity culture certainly picks up the slack.

If Nature hasn't been generous to a French person, he or she will very often use Art. Plastic surgery in France is a booming growth industry, with almost five times more people resorting to surgical procedures than in Britain.

The following advertisement comes from the website

of one of Paris's most popular and exclusive *clubs échangistes*, or swingers' clubs: 'Seduction is an art to be cultivated. We are players in the game of seduction. No excuses! If you no longer seduce, look in your mirror for your mirror is truthful . . . We propose that you pamper yourself, look after your body. We invite you to use a thousand artifices: clothes, make-up, jewellery, wigs . . . We love you feminine, elegant, refined, coquettish, provocative . . .'

It is hard to imagine anything so openly sexist being written in English today. But in France, the somewhat archaic idea that women are endlessly mysterious and fascinating creatures whose role is to sexually intoxicate men still holds sway. The sexual protocol in clubs like these remains pretty close to what it must have been in the eighteenth century. An English journalist, who went to a *club échangiste* in order to write about it for his broadsheet, described the experience of walking into one of the elegant back rooms where a naked woman was tied, blindfolded, to silken manacles on the wall: 'It was like walking into a chapel. A few men and women were pleasuring her while the rest were watching in what can only be described as total awe.'

Only a certain ritual, or what the French call *mise en scène*, can promote this kind of atmosphere. The 'contractual' nature of relationships between men and women in Britain and the resulting de-sexualisation has made it difficult to return to these primal roles, and so the kind of religious awe the English journalist was describing becomes more and more difficult to achieve. These unchanged stereotypes in an otherwise changed world create a paradoxically innocent atmosphere. There is an elegance and a decorum in Paris's swingers' clubs that makes them remarkably unthreatening. Laurent, who has been a few times with various girlfriends, described meeting a business acquaintance whom he met sipping champagne with a scantily clad woman at the bar.

'We acknowledged each other politely and that was it. There was no embarrassment. It was like meeting in a parallel universe. It will never be mentioned again.'

While we were together Laurent soon gave up trying to convince me to go with him to a swingers' club. He knew that with my background, our evening would never be light-hearted, fun, anecdotal. With my insecurities and my puritan guilt, the experience would only become tawdry and complicated.

I came to France wearing the uniform of my generation: pink, spiky hair, mohair jumper pulled down over a tartan mini-skirt, fishnet tights and Doc Martens. After a year in Paris living under the gentle but persistent influence of Laurent and his entourage, I had been radically remodelled. In my sock drawer, silk underwear and stockings had supplanted fluorescent tights and stripy socks. While my English girlfriends continued to hide their figures under multiple layers, I was undergoing a slow conversion to the French cult of appearances. For many years I resisted the change – periodically 'regressing' to clothes that I could hide in, or as my husband's friend Gilles would put it, clothes that chopped me up into 'unflattering sections'. It was Gilles whom my husband had left, that first summer, in charge of taking me shopping.

'Ma chérie,' Gilles said as we walked down the rue du Jour one afternoon in July. 'This "poor English girl" look has to go. You should enjoy your figure [*plastique*] and let other people enjoy it as well.'

At the time his words encapsulated everything that an earnest young woman like me despised: snobbishness, superficiality and sexism. Today I can see a certain generosity of outlook. His remarks were not about sex or politics but about the nature of Beauty. In his view, whatever shape God had given me needed to be adorned and embellished for my own enjoyment and for that of others. Clothes, he believed, were not tribal dress, designed to flag our position on the social grid. They were there at the service of Beauty and should be used to emphasise certain elements of a person's physique and to de-emphasise others.

Gilles had used the word *plastique* (from the Greek word *plassein*, to mould). This word perfectly conveys the various assumptions that lie behind his observation. When used as a noun with a feminine indefinite article, *plastique* refers to the beauty inherent in shape. The example for the definition given in the Le Robert dictionary is *Cette femme a une plastique étonnante*. Translated into English the sentence loses its meaning: That woman has a formal beauty that is striking. Since the noun *plastique* invariably tends to be used for a woman, it expresses the French belief that the female form is inherently beautiful.

All of this should help to understand why the French tend to be conservative in their dress. Clothes at the service of Beauty don't draw attention to themselves or to the personality of the wearer but to the *plastique* or particular beauty – whatever it may be – of the rack they're adorning.

A Frenchman will never tell a woman she looks 'well' when what he means is that she looks beautiful or radiant or sexy. Nor indeed will a woman. I remember how thrilled or appalled my girlfriends could be when Laurent used to greet them. He would always mention how lovely they were looking, and the genuine delight in his face usually disarmed them.

Ella, my twenty-year-old daughter, has been brought up in France. She says that London makes her feel sad and ugly. In Paris she no longer notices male attention, but in London she notices its absence: no smiles, no catcalls, no homage whatsoever to her youth and beauty.

'Nobody looks at each other here,' she once remarked as we stepped off the London tube. 'It's not just the men, women don't look at each other either.'

'It's rude to stare,' I said, unconvincingly.

But for Ella, of course, it was rude to be ignored.

3 Being a Woman

La Libido, La Femme Fatale and the Sisterhood

The cults of Pleasure and Beauty are allegedly why French
women don't get fat. This, of course, is simply not true.
There are plenty of fat French women about and as fast-
food invades France, they're getting more and more
numerous.* But because there is no sin attached either to
the pleasure of sex or to the pleasure of food, overeating
tends not to be a manifestation of self-loathing. Put simply, if your body is a temple for the pursuit of guilt-free
sexual pleasures, then you're less likely to want to trash it.

I, like most women in France, have a gynaecologist.
When I first arrived, my mother-in-law, Madeleine, had
insisted on it. The French gynaecologist is usually a self-
appointed sexologist as well. Every time I went for a
check-up my gynaecologist would look up from his notes
and, with an earnest expression, ask me:

'*Et la libido? Ça va?*'

Once, I admitted that things were a bit sluggish in that
department.

'How long have you been married? Eight years? *C'est*

* Obese people make up almost 10 per cent of the population in
France versus over 20 per cent in the UK.

normal. I can give you a little testosterone if you like.'

He then warned me that it might produce a little unwanted hair but that it worked wonders.

I told him that I'd leave it for the time being.

Even French GPs concern themselves with their patients' sexual health. An English friend of mine who has been living in Paris for five years recently went to his GP for a check-up. In the middle of the consultation, there was a knock on the door. The doctor's secretary begged to be excused for the interruption. She had a patient on the phone who was complaining that she hadn't had an orgasm for a month and she wondered if it could be the result of the medication the doctor had prescribed. My friend watched the doctor in disbelief as he pondered the matter for a moment.

'*Non, non.* It's not the medication. It's probably psychological factors. Tell her she can make an appointment to discuss it.'

The secretary smiled sweetly at my friend and then closed the door behind her. Without the slightest ripple of unease, the GP picked up where he had left off.

There is an entire sub-genre within the canon of French cinema that deals with the subject of frigidity. When I first arrived, Laurent was always taking me to see these films, the first of which was one of his favourites: *L'Eté Meurtrier*, with Isabelle Adjani. This film is also part of the category known as *Femme Fatale* films, for which the French seem to have an inexhaustible appetite. In the film

Adjani plays a tragically frigid, pouting beauty who seeks revenge for the rape of her mother by marrying and mentally torturing the son of one of the supposed rapists. The film, set in a picturesque village in Provence in the mid-seventies, is a vehicle for Adjani's lithe and permanently sweaty body. At the time I couldn't believe that my new husband, a man who had three university degrees, could actually fall for such drivel. Now, when I see the film, I'm struck by how accurately it portrays French provincial life – a certain turn of phrase, a certain era and a certain type of French woman, who really does exist. French women do pout. Widespread pouting among women is a reflection of the belief that women are allowed to, expected to, behave badly. (It is also a fact that the French language – with its reliance on the various forms of the short 'o' and 'u' sound – is set up for pouting.)

Pouting is also the speciality of the *femme-enfant*, a label that would be highly inappropriate in Britain but which has wide currency as a compliment in France. The term would probably translate into English as 'bimbo', losing all positive connotation in the process. For the French, on the other hand, Brigitte Bardot was the classic *femme-enfant*, and the scene which best depicts this feminine ideal is the opening moments in Jean-Luc Godard's 1963 film *Le Mépris* (Contempt) in which Bardot lies naked on the bed and asks her lover which part of her body he likes best. The refrain 'And my feet, do you like my feet? And my breasts, do you like my breasts? Which do you prefer, my nipples or my breasts?', the monumen-

tal stupidity of Bardot, comes across in France as irresistible coquetry. In French she sounds sexy; in English,
like an overgrown and deranged toddler.

Another classic that Laurent took me to see was *Le
Septième Ciel* (Seventh Heaven), by Benoît Jacquot. It's
about a woman called Mathilde who cannot reach
orgasm. To solve her problem she goes to see a hypnotist.
The hypnosis works and she goes home to her husband
and her climax wakes up the neighbours. Betty, a girlfriend with whom I discussed the film, informed me that I
was wrong, that the story wasn't at all implausible. Plenty
of Parisian women, she explained, went to hypnotists to
help them relax enough to come, and if I liked she could
give me the number for hers, a very nice man (though
with bad breath) whose practice was near the Place de la
République.

Having been brought up in post-feminist Britain, it took
me almost a decade to adjust to the experience of being a
woman in France. Since France seemed to have been
bypassed by the feminist revolution, women appeared to
me woefully un-emancipated, still pitted against each
other and trapped in the archaic patriarchal model of sexual competition. They seemed to have no interest in
friendship and would invariably gaze past me at parties
when I tried to engage them in conversation, as if they
were watching a world of erotic opportunity disappearing
down the plughole. Often I would come home after such
evenings and cry on my husband's shoulder. I missed

England and above all, I missed my female friendships.

My eldest sister, Florence, after ten years in Paris, had fled her younger sisters a second time and gone to live in Manhattan. Irene and I hardly ever saw each other. She had moved with her French husband to a chic suburb to the west of Paris and I found myself repeatedly bowing to Laurent's bourgeois Parisian reluctance to cross the *périphérique* (Paris's ring road) to visit her. Over the years, Irene and I developed opposing techniques to cope with our homesickness. Irene made a haven of Englishness for herself and her Anglophile husband. They spoke to each other in English, listened to Radio 4, watched English football on satellite TV and, when their children were born, employed an English-speaking nanny to look after them. I, on the other hand, slowly but surely and much to Irene's amusement would, as she would put it, *go native*.

Recently, I had lunch with Hortense, one of those Parisian women whom I had found so icy and who has, over the years, become my friend. She was interested to hear that she had terrified me when I first met her, and that she had seemed disdainful and unapproachable. She smiled.

'You frightened *me*,' she said. 'You were so . . . open, so different.'

Her hazel eyes shone with affection. I've known her for twenty years and she has changed very little. She still has the same mass of shiny, beautifully blow-dried hair, the youthful spattering of freckles across the nose and the same (pouting) mouth.

'It was the role we had to play,' she explained. '*La femme fatale*. You have to remember that here the pleasure all lies in the business of being a woman. That's where real life is played out, in our love affairs. Nowhere else. There's really not much difference between the life of a *bourgeoise* like me and the life of a courtesan.'

'But you've been more than that. You did a brilliant degree. You've got a high-powered job.'

'Still. My energies all went elsewhere. We were brought up to be, above all, seductive. We put on our high heels and our make-up to go to Sciences Po and we hunted for men among the elite.'

'How exhausting.'

'Sometimes. But it's in us. We can't be any different. We have an obligation to our femininity. In our company a man should feel like a man. There should always be a spark of mystery.'

'And what about as you get older? Do you still have to go on doing this in your fifties and sixties?'

'Actually, it gets easier. You learn to wear only what suits you and you use what you have.'

'Do you wish things were different?'

She leaned towards me, lowering her voice.

'*It was fun.*' Then she added, 'In theory, of course, love affairs should just be the icing on the cake. They shouldn't define you but they do. They take up so much *time*.'

She paused.

'The trouble is, of course, you dwell in appearances.'

'And we all lose our looks,' I said.

She smiled mischievously.

'Men lose their looks too. You must just take a younger lover.'

Even though I knew the answer, I asked her if she had had affairs.

'Many,' she said.

'And your husband?'

'I don't know. I don't want to know.'

'Do most of your girlfriends have affairs?'

'Yes. I would say that most of the couples that we know are unfaithful to each other. There is a tradition of *libertinage* in my *milieu*, which is very strong. It's in our literature, our theatre and our cinema. Of course there is guilt. I never want to hurt my husband but a love affair is irresistible. I don't *want* to resist it.'

I will never share with Hortense the intimacy and camaraderie that I share with my English girlfriends. There is an ease among both British and American women that is the direct result of the lack of rivalry. Because of the archaic, unreconstructed nature of gender politics in France, women still perceive each other as rivals in the game of love. I know that for Hortense her love affairs come first, that she wouldn't hesitate to cancel me in favour of an assignation. This is understood. With the sisterhood in England and America, things are different. We're taught to put our female friendships first, or at least make sure that we appear to do so.

I think of Aurélie, the sex goddess, and remember how

terrified I was by her erotic legacy in the early days of my marriage. To me she embodied everything that I mistrusted about the French woman. Her agenda was seduction and all her energies seemed to go in that direction. She seemed to have no female friendships at all and always seemed to be stealing other people's husbands or boyfriends. When I discovered, over dinner in a restaurant with Laurent, the manner in which their affair had begun, all my worst fears were confirmed.

Aurélie was the girlfriend of one of Laurent's oldest friends, Robert, a photographer who would become godfather to our first child. After they had been together for about two years, Aurélie found herself suddenly and irresistibly attracted to her boyfriend's best mate, Laurent. Laurent had recently taken up running first thing in the morning in the Bois de Boulogne, close to where he worked. Aurélie asked if she might join him. Laurent described to me over dinner how she had made her move on him:

'She stopped to rest against a tree. She was panting, her insolent little breasts [I remember he used the word *narquois* for those breasts, meaning, literally, mocking] heaving up and down under her tiny vest . . . She was staring at me and panting, waiting for me to jump on her. I couldn't resist.'

This is the French woman's way: you *never* make the first move, but you try to make it impossible for the man *not* to. Judging from a conversation that I would have years later with my own daughter, this is still the approach of the Parisian female. Ella had recently returned from a weekend in London, where she had been to a party given by the daughter of a friend of mine. Her description of the dance floor took me back to my own adolescence: all those lovely, strong females dancing together in the middle of the room and all those insecure, faltering males hovering around the edge as if repelled by the contrapuntal force of the girls' erotic empowerment. Apparently, Ella tried the waiting game she usually plays at parties in Paris and the boys all ignored her.

Laurent went on to tell me how poor Robert, six months later, discovered his affair with Aurélie. They and a group of friends were having dinner together in a big, noisy brasserie off the Place de la Bastille. Aurélie was sitting beside her official boyfriend and opposite her lover. When Robert bent down to pick up his lighter, he saw his girlfriend's foot comfortably nestled where it shouldn't be and that was that. She moved out of Robert's flat and in with Laurent. It is a measure of the banality of adultery here that Laurent and Robert – and indeed Aurélie – are still firm friends.

When I heard this story I inwardly vowed to cut Aurélie out of my life. At the time Laurent had the elegance not to object, but after we had split up he and Aurélie became close again. Today I feel a good deal more charitable towards her. In fact, as Hortense once explained to me, women like Aurélie fulfil a useful role in society. They are erotic catalysts. Not all women should be matronly or sisterly or otherwise sexually passive. If they are, the erotic charge disappears from the social group, or goes underground and becomes pathological, disembodied, infected by guilt. The idea is that in the presence of this type of predatory woman, wives and girlfriends feel at risk and this sense of risk reboots the libido. Significantly, Carl Jung identified the vital social role of this type of woman in his book *Aspects of the Feminine*. Even he, however, could not help giving her the pejorative label 'The Overdeveloped Eros'.

There is no 'sisterhood' in France and for many years this was something I missed profoundly. With time, however, I realised – as I did of most areas of French life – that in losing one thing I had found another. I learnt that the extraordinary female friendships I had known in Britain were part of a wider landscape, itself not so pretty – a landscape ravaged by a low-level and persistent war between the sexes. The absence of gender conflict in France has become a source of relief to me. Once I had overcome my prejudices, I realised that the constant flirtation – often heavy-handed and irritating but sometimes subtle and uplifting – was a pretty harmless thing compared to the deep-seated resentment that seems to infect gender relations in Britain. There is no tradition of gender segregation in France because men enjoy the company of women. Stag parties are a recent aberration imported by Anglophiles, and the gentleman's club is reserved for a tiny proportion of the French aristocracy that enjoys aping the English. There is no such thing here as a 'ladette' because French women are happy to be admired for their femininity.

I had imagined that the hostility between the sexes in Britain began with feminism, but I now think that it must have been a much longer-standing feature of British life. You only have to look back to seventeenth-century Jacobean tragedy to find evidence of an already entrenched and elaborate misogyny that was absent from French courtly drama. From as early as the fourteenth century, British women had become targets of male animosity as they found ways of engaging in Britain's emerging market economy, mostly as manufacturers and sellers of goods. France's Salic Law (which barred female heirs from the throne) and her enduring chivalric tradition – whose values were perpetuated by the French court – kept French women in a subordinate position, shielding them from male resentment.* It may be that it was simply England's mercantile culture that shaped the special blend of chumminess and competition that seems to characterise

---

* In France, right up to the Napoleonic Code, a woman was subject to the authority of her father and then her husband, almost to the exclusion of any economic freedom. On marrying, the husband and wife's assets were automatically combined, and the husband administered this joint estate without the wife's consent. The Napoleonic Marital Code brought in a new era of economic independence, at least for wealthy women. It provided for the possibility of a pre-nuptial agreement, which kept the wife's assets separate from her husband's. If a wife chose to combine her assets with those of her husband, he was legally accountable to her in the disposal of their fortune. It wasn't until 1882 under the Married Women's Property Act

male–female relations in Britain and America. For feminism, when it came, sat far better in our two Protestant cultures than it ever could in France's Catholic one.

The cross-gender tension that permeates both British and American society is not easy to describe, precisely because it is everywhere. In England, at least, I can feel it at dinner parties, on the radio, on the street. An unspoken agenda seems to exist between men and women in Anglo-Saxon Protestant societies that produces a certain carefulness in men – or else an irritating defiance – and in women, a kind of guardedness, brittleness, even a sanctimoniousness. I have noticed that the tension is often camouflaged by that chumminess, which is not only unsexy but also slightly disingenuous. I'm not suggesting that men and women hate each other in Britain or America any more or less than they do in France, only that there is a lack of ease in their relations that is the direct result of having tried – and to some degree succeeded – in extending the rules of our contractual, mercantile society to the sexual playing field. In our otherwise laudable quest for transparency, we have managed to sabotage one of the greatest pleasures of life: the experience of enjoying being a woman in the company of a man or a man in the company of a woman. In Britain and America this pleasure has become shot through with a whole new kind of post-

---

that British married women gained access to similar freedoms as their French sisters. Thanks also to Napoleon, French daughters were given the same inheritance rights as their brothers, while England's primogeniture laws remained intact until 1925.

feminist guilt, and no one, it seems – neither man nor woman – is entirely free of it.

I'm also struck by the frequency with which public and private discourse in both Britain and America returns to the issue of gender, like an itch that has to be scratched. At least as a concept, to be endlessly discussed and scrutinised, gender doesn't really exist in France. Indeed, the French word *genre*, meaning gender, is a purely grammatical or literary term. (It is, I think, significant that if you want to talk in French about gender politics you have to use the words 'man' and 'woman': *les relations hommes–femmes*.)

Even though Simone de Beauvoir inaugurated a flourishing and highly intellectual feminist tradition in France, and even though many of the mothers of feminist theory are of French nationality or culture (Luce Irigaray, Hélène Cixous, Julia Kristeva*), anyone wishing to take a course in Women's Studies would probably have to do so outside of France, as it exists in only one, small department of one university. In France, the representation of women in society can be studied as *part* of a course in literature or philosophy or history or psychoanalysis or sociology, but it cannot be cut off from a wider cultural and intellectual context. Although French intellectuals, men and women, were among the first to scrutinise cultural representations of gender, the practice of decoding the myriad power

---

* All three of these women would probably refer to themselves as psychoanalysts or philosophers rather than feminist thinkers. Indeed, they might even require a definition of that label before agreeing to it.

struggles that exist between men and women has not become the national pastime that it is in Britain. The French are too romantic for that, even the most seemingly hard-nosed of them. Perhaps the fixation with gender politics is simply puritan Britain's way of taking the sex out of sexuality.

I am convinced that the reason I notice this low-level hostility in Britain is because I do not encounter it in the place where I live. In France, the war between the sexes simply never got off the ground. Somehow, social evolution has brought about changes to the status of women without ever giving men the impression that they were *losing* something in the process. French women also happen to be very attached to the particular privileges that have always gone with being a woman – privileges the Catholic Church cleverly conferred upon them over the centuries in exchange for their submission. While they are just as eager to secure their social and political rights as their British sisters, they do not wish to give up the experience of being loved for their beauty, sexual power, mystique or indeed any other of the often illusory qualities for which they are admired.

While the struggle for women's rights continues to rage in France, it is as if there has been an unspoken pact to keep Eros out of the fray, the received wisdom being that you cannot regulate the bedroom. France's version of the feminist revolution left untouched the private roles that men and women played. It was only in academic circles that traditional feminine archetypes were deconstructed in the name of equality. These archetypes, which all centre on the notion of power, exercised or relinquished – and are the stuff that the libido thrives on – remain intact in the private sphere. For in this culture, the libido is not only fun, it is sacred.

4 Truth versus Beauty

Tragedy, Comedy and Historic French Losers

It did not take me long to realise that the French inhabit a different moral universe to ours, a universe that clearly placed the pursuit of Pleasure and Beauty above notions of Truth and Duty. One episode and its aftermath offered a perfect illustration of the gap between our two world views.

It was the final of the 2006 World Cup. The French football team had clawed its way from mediocrity to brilliance to find itself in a tantalisingly close final against the Italians. For Zinédine Zidane, undisputed hero of French football, it was the last game of a flawless career. With minutes to go before the final whistle Zidane turned on the Italian defender, Marco Materazzi, and delivered a powerful head-butt to the man's chest, knocking him to the ground. Denounced by the linesman, Zidane received a red card and was sent off. Fans watched him walk, head bowed, past the World Cup trophy on its stand, and disappear into the changing rooms. In his absence, the French lost to the Italians in a penalty shoot-out.

In Britain the next day the *Sun*'s headline was 'Zidane's a hero to Zzero'. For Alan Shearer 'It was just a moment of madness', and for the BBC football pundit, Alan

Hansen, 'He let himself down, he let his team down and he let his country down.'

Back in France a very different debate was taking shape, the tone of which was set by the then president, Jacques Chirac, interviewed at the end of the match. 'I don't know what happened,' the president lied, but Zinédine Zidane 'possesses the greatest human qualities that can be imagined and which are an honour to France'.

The French media began to speculate, as did the rest of the world, on the exact nature of Materazzi's taunt. Professional lip-readers were hired to decipher whether or not the Italian had insulted Zidane's sick mother or his wife, called him a terrorist or a dirty Arab. But while the British press referred unequivocally to Zidane's 'shameful' act, the French press was much more careful in apportioning blame. However rash Zidane's gesture had been, shameful was clearly not an appropriate adjective. The one thing that was *not* up for discussion was Zidane's heroic nature. To respond rashly to injury is not shaming. Zizou had merely shown himself to be *human*, as President Chirac had wisely put it.

What was broadly agreed was that with this stunning act of self-sabotage, the final touch had been added to Zizou's hagiography. He was human. In other words, his crime was nothing more or less than *hubris*. Or as the daily newspaper *Libération* put it: 'In destroying the dream that he himself had created, Zidane remained unfathomable to the end. For some, his gesture verged on the sublime.'

For the French, Zidane had, in that poignant moment when he walked off the pitch and turned his back on glory, become a tragic hero. Asked in a television interview if he would have changed his career's end if he could, Zidane answered: 'No. It was decided *upstairs* that this was going to be my end.' Then he added, 'I've always tried to be honest, I'm just a human being with all the weaknesses.'

An interesting parenthesis to the story of the Fall of Zidane is that he was, at the time of the insult, having an affair with a young singer. He and the young woman had been photographed together by one of the newly emerging tabloid magazines, *People* (pronounced 'Pipol'), but the mainstream press had dutifully avoided the story – *jardin secret oblige*. Materazzi had apparently insulted Zidane's wife and, by extension, his honour. For the general public, to whom Zidane's liaison with the lovely young singer was widely known, there was no hypocrisy in the footballer's sense of outrage. A wife is still sacred, even if you happen to be cheating on her. As for the matter of the Truth, the French – as I would soon learn – do not hold the virtue of truth in such high esteem as the British.

The day after the World Cup final, President Chirac invited the French team to the Elysée Palace and addressed Zidane directly in the following words: 'Dear Zinédine Zidane, what I have to say to you at this intense moment, perhaps the hardest moment of your career, is all the admiration and affection of a whole nation; its respect too . . . You are a virtuoso, a genius of world football. You are also a man of the heart, a man of commitment, engagement and conviction. And that is why France admires and loves you.'

The key, then, is not winning, nor is it – as our Protestant mythology likes to claim – the joy of simply participating. France loves men like Zidane for their commitment, their virtuosity and their *panache*, not for their success. Traits like rigour, reserve and resilience – qualities which, significantly, are usually attributed to France's Protestant minority – are begrudgingly admired but never championed. Only the great losers of history repeatedly capture the imaginations of French writers and filmmakers: figures like Joan of Arc, Napoleon and the martyr of the French resistance, Jean Moulin.

France and her history are tuned to a tragic register. Every one of her regimes – monarchies and empires included – right up until the Fifth Republic, ended in bloodshed, rebellion or catastrophe. Tragedy is her element. Britain, with her tradition of political compromise and her attachment to the durability of custom, is more at ease with the comic.

The French are not. They're not, as we know, at all funny; they rarely understand irony and they're never, ever self-deprecating. They are too *involved*, too committed for comedy, too busy *feeling*.

Of comedy the philosopher Henri Bergson said in his essay on laughter, *Le Rire: Essai sur la Signification du Comique*: 'Indifference is its natural element. There is no greater enemy to emotion than laughter.'

The comic view requires a certain detachment from life and its vicissitudes, something of which the French are quite incapable. Even the French language – with its paucity of nouns and their multitudes of meaning – is more emotionally charged than English. I recently went to see a production of *Krapp's Last Tape*, a play that Samuel Beckett wrote initially in English, and then translated into French. The director had been granted permission by the notoriously finicky Beckett estate to put on the two versions of this one-man show back to back. First we sat through the French version then the English, each one acted in strict accordance with Beckett's precise and plentiful stage directions. In spite of there being little or no variation between the performances, the play, as it moved from French to English, shifted imperceptibly from a tragic to a blackly comic register.

The comic view is also one that looks at reality between the eyes and dares to describe it. Comedy rolls around in the nitty-gritty of reality, while tragedy seeks escape through ideas. The French love of the tragic view of life goes hand in hand with their love of ideas.

Comedy is the resource of the long-suffering. For the British, it is an antidote to the various hardships associated with living on a damp, windy island in the North Sea. Our humour has been honed and crafted over centuries. The easier people have it, it seems, the less their need for comedy. Today, France's only decent stand-up comedians are her outcasts and fringe-dwellers – her Arabs and her North African Jews.

The French, who have a horror of appearing stupid, tend to prefer wit to humour, and so the one has thrived to the detriment of the other. I was struck, when I first arrived in Paris, by how totally lacking in silliness dinner-party conversation was. I was stunned to find that people – even young people – thought that punning was funny; I would watch the gay rallying of *jeux de mots* in amazement. As the years went by, I entertained myself by becoming sillier, until it grew apparent that I had become *l'Anglaise de service*, a kind of clown, reliably irreverent and accommodatingly dippy.

France, in the eighties, seemed to me a comic desert. When I discovered, from his domination of prime-time television, that for most French viewers English humour meant Benny Hill, I was even more horrified. Today Mr Bean has replaced Benny Hill in the hearts of French comedy-lovers. On the one or two occasions that I made the mistake of trusting my French friends enough to bring out the latest example of English or American comedy, I have been met with stunned incomprehension. When my own children, thrilled by the prospect of a relaxed evening's entertainment with their friends, brought back an Eddie Izzard DVD from London, they had to accept the chasm that existed between their humour and that of their peers.

'But why does he dress like a woman? Drag isn't funny any more . . .' said one.

'The gags are too long-winded . . .' said another.

Unable to explain that being in drag was not the point

and that being long-winded was, my two children gave up and now confine themselves to clandestine comedy-viewing with their English cousins.

Television, Hypocrisy and Ideas

There is something contrary about the French; something that the English often perceive as perverse. But this *awkwardness* is the stuff of which French identity is made. It is born of the perpetual and irreconcilable confrontation between *the idea* and *the reality*.

Recently I asked a French friend, a former English teacher and enthusiastic Anglophile, what it was that she liked about the English. Her answer goes a long way towards explaining what it is that I have found most difficult about living in France.

'In England', she said, 'I learnt that it was possible to be more than one thing.' When I pressed her for an explanation, she answered, 'In English society a person can be complex, hold contradictory positions and ideas. In France, because of our idealism and our history, we are encouraged to take sides, and this can be very boring.'

To my mother-in-law, Madeleine, and to a great many French people, the dominant characteristic of the English is their alleged hypocrisy. Indeed, the expression *l'hypocrisie anglaise* refers to what the French see as our perfidious habit of dissimulation. It does not occur to them that where they see duplicity may simply be doubt, nor that our unwillingness to take a stand might not be a posture but a genuine state of mind. In French, the words 'equivocal' or 'ambivalent' both carry the negative connotation of moral ambiguity before they convey the more neutral idea of multiplicity of meaning. Once again, as experts on the vicissitudes of reality over ideas, the British are aware that nothing is as simple as it seems.

A good example of this confusion between pragmatism and duplicity can be found in French accounts of the personality of Oliver Cromwell, a man endlessly puzzling to the French. As leader of the English Revolution, Cromwell should have been an idealist. His life and actions proved him to have been quite the opposite and so for the French, he must have been a hypocrite.

Drawn to the complexities of Cromwell's character, Victor Hugo combed through countless seventeenth-century pamphlets and newspapers in the course of writing an interminable and rarely performed play about him. In the play, Cromwell is characterised as a parliamentarian who dreams of becoming a monarch. This Romantic conceit works perfectly well in French. The idea that the epitome of moral complexity is the figure of a man in whom two conflicting ideas are constantly vying for supremacy would have served perfectly the character of Napoleon, with his legendary histrionics. But Cromwell was an Englishman, and therefore not necessarily required to be consistent or even coherent. John Buchan beautifully described Cromwell's paradoxical nature in his 1934 biography and at no point judged him for it: 'A devotee of law, he was forced to be often lawless; a civilian to the core, he had to maintain himself by the sword; with a passion to construct, his task was chiefly to destroy; the most scrupulous of men, he had to ride roughshod over his own scruples and those of others; the tenderest, he had continually to harden his heart; the most English of our greater figures, he spent his life in opposition to the majority of Englishmen; a realist, he was condemned to build that which could not last.'

For the French, complexity very quickly becomes hypocrisy. Bishop Bossuet, the scourge and converter of Protestants under Louis XIV, described Cromwell as 'a man of an incredible depth of mind, a refined hypocrite as well as a skilled politician'.* Recent French scholarship on the man hardly differs in its interpretation: 'As much as his political acumen, Cromwell owed his success to his profound hypocrisy.'†

This confusion explains the strange mixture of admiration and contempt with which the French judge the English character. When they call Oliver Cromwell a hypocrite, they are not referring to any gap between what he might have practised and what he preached. Hypocrisy in French does not necessarily infer the pretence of virtue, which is a person's private affair, but rather an excess of complexity, a lack of moral *readability*.

The French need to know at all times whose side you are on, which – for an English person – can become very tedious.

*

* Bishop Jacques-Benigne Bossuet, *Sermon for the Funeral of Queen Henrietta* (1669).
† Cromwell's entry in *Imago Mundi*, French online encyclopaedia.

The French love of ideas has had a devastating effect on the independence and quality of her media. Television was seen from the outset as a hugely powerful vehicle for ideas, and the habit of presidential meddling is a long-established tradition that has been hard to break. France's two most influential newspapers, *Le Monde* and *Le Figaro*, were basically created – or in the case of *Le Figaro*, re-created – after the Occupation by de Gaulle, and in his own image. From as early as 1944, in his configuration of France's post-traumatic political landscape, the general was animated by a deep mistrust of communism. Forced – by the legitimacy conferred by their Resistance credentials – to compose a government with communist ministers, de Gaulle was careful to make sure that French radio and newspapers fell into the hands of his political allies. Driven by his dual mistrust of communism and the Americans, de Gaulle also created a new daily newspaper – *Le Monde* – and named his Resistance buddy, Hubert Beuve Méry, as its editor. It was Beuve Méry who said on the eve of the Allied landings: 'The Americans constitute a real danger to France. They can stop a necessary revolution and their materialism does not have the tragic grandeur of the totalitarian regimes.' Once again, at the heart of this quite widespread anti-American sentiment, lies the conviction that Anglo-Saxon culture is basely materialistic and lacking in grandeur. It is this very sentiment, this love of so-called 'tragic grandeur' that led legions of French intellectuals to support two of the worst totalitarian regimes in history –

Mao's and Stalin's – long after everyone else had woken up to their horrors.

Just like *Le Monde*, the modern-day *Le Figaro* was intentionally partisan. The paper reappeared in 1944, after a two-year hiatus under the Nazi Occupation. This right-leaning daily newspaper, in existence since 1826, became the official mouthpiece of the newly founded political party the MRP, which had its roots in the Christian branches of the Resistance. On 25 August 1944 its first edition opened with a eulogistic editorial by François Mauriac on de Gaulle. This politicisation of the press, born out of the trauma of collaboration and the dangerous instability of post-war France, has meant that there is no lasting tradition of independence in the media. It also goes some way towards explaining the paucity of investigative journalism. Since de Gaulle, Presidents Mitterrand, Chirac and even Sarkozy, when he was minister of the interior, are all known to have picked up their phones to have someone sacked from a TV station or newspaper.

Alain Peyrefitte, formerly de Gaulle's minister of information, gives a telling account in his brilliant and unflinching study of his own countrymen, *Le Mal Français*, of just how deeply involved the French government is in controlling the media. He describes being led into his new office in 1962 and his predecessor proudly showing him a row of buttons on his desk – given the times, it would probably have looked like something from *Thunderbirds* – and saying: 'That one is to summon the porter, that one your secretary, that one gets you through to the head of

RTF [National Radio and Television], that one to the news editor for radio and television, and those two to heads of programming for radio and for television . . .'

It is hard to imagine, even as far back as 1962, a British government minister calling the editor of BBC radio or television news every evening at five o'clock and giving him the order for the day. But this is what happened in France and continued, more or less openly, and despite Alain Peyrefitte's efforts to the contrary, right up into the early years of Mitterrand's presidency.

Living in a society with no real tradition of independent media has one advantage: no one takes the media seriously and, as a result, its influence is extremely limited. Unlike the British, the French do not sit around and talk about what they have seen on TV, which is seen as a simplistic and implausible medium. It is rare that millions of French people will be held captive by a television programme; there is no equivalent to the numbers of viewers drawn by *EastEnders*, *Big Brother* or *The Apprentice*. France is not a society that sits huddled around its TV screens.

Television is also, of course, a medium naturally given to the worship of reality. In line with our love of reality and our taste for the comic over the tragic, the British are excellent watchers and makers of television. The French, on the other hand, with their love of grand ideas and their contempt for reality, make execrable television. Hours of French airtime are devoted to the spectacle of people (anybody will do) sitting around discussing ideas. There is none of the British mistrust of 'talking heads'. Talking heads are seen as a good thing in France, and the louder they talk the better.

The extent to which the British nation recognises itself in its television is unimaginable to French people, for whom TV is and always has been an inferior medium. People in Britain are happy to devote hours of their leisure time to watching or discussing television, and the BBC is an object of national pride. The same is not true of TF1 or France Télévisions, or even the relatively new window on mainstream bourgeois culture, Canal+. The amazing diversity and inventiveness of British TV make it possible for the British public to identify massively with its output. In France no such consensus is possible. French television is not a mirror of the French soul and French people do not recognise themselves in their TV, radio, nor indeed in their newspapers. The result is that there is no media bandwagon here. People in France are not animated, in unison, by the same obsessions and anxieties as we are in Britain, where one week it's cot-death syndrome, the next it's paedophiles, the next it's binge-drinking – the whole nation tilting like so many sunflowers to wherever our media shines its mighty beam. There is a paradoxical feeling associated with this concordance: on the one hand, it's a comforting sensation of being part of a small, cosy island in which we all vibrate together – to the strike of Big Ben, to the theme tunes of *Big Brother*, *Coronation Street*, *The Archers* – and, on the other, an oppressive, claustrophobic feeling that makes many Britons long to escape.

The absence of consensus in France explains, in part, French conformism. When I first arrived I was struck by the general partiality to navy blue or beige. Even young people standing outside their *lycées* seemed all to look the same. I was puzzled by the conservatism of my own children's dress as they were growing up.

'Why, when you don't have to wear a uniform, don't you dress a bit more crazily?'

They had no wish to dress crazily or stand out in any way. They wanted the same rucksack (Eastpack was the brand and still is) as everyone else; the same jeans, the same stationery. In the absence of rules, they made their own, expressing French society's tendency to bow to a dominant cultural model rather than to form a willing consensus.

It is a strange paradox that my children, with all their apparent conformism, their desire to fit in and their willingness to look like everyone else, do not suffer any of the feelings of mental constraint or moral claustrophobia that I have described. They clearly *feel* free, even if they aren't, and this sensation (or illusion) is key to the French identity. How free do the British feel, or indeed how free do we care to feel? Perhaps to the British, Freedom is as overrated as Truth is to the French.

5 The Wedding

Catholicism, Anti-Semitism and Le Pen

Laurent and I were married in a small seventeenth-century church in Normandy. In the first of three cursory meetings the priest had asked me to promise to raise my children as Catholics. I don't know if it was the man's halitosis or my religious convictions that made me so uncharacteristically resolute, but I explained that I couldn't make such a promise. Laurent, who as a perfect atheist was only going through the whole rigmarole to please his parents, didn't intervene. He sat with his arms folded while the priest and I did our best to reach a compromise. In the end it was agreed that I would promise, when the time came, to offer our children the choice of taking their First Holy Communion.

The French Catholic Church has a long experience of deal-making. Forced to cohabit with what remained of the more unchristian values of Roman, then courtly society – the code of honour being paramount among those values – French Catholicism is no stranger to compromise. Although France today is no longer Catholic in any sense but culturally, that culture of compromise is still deeply entrenched. It was as if the Church knew that if it were to survive, it would have to make religious practice as undemanding and as compatible with the requirements of secular life as possible.

There is no doubt that when France chose to turn her back on the Reformation and remain Catholic – despite the fact that her king, Henri IV de Navarre, and much of her aristocracy had converted to the new faith – she chose the path of least resistance. The Protestant relationship with the deity would always be the more difficult: no intermediary in the shape of a corruptible priest, only your conscience to guide you, the relentless scrutiny of the rest of the congregation and, above all, no confessional to wash you of your misdemeanours. There is no doubt that Catholicism, with all its rituals and suspended disbelief, knew how to reel in the masses. No matter how uncompromising the edicts from the Vatican, the French Catholic Church has always been, in practice, remarkably tolerant of sin. You only have to compare attitudes in Britain and France towards adultery, the most banal sin of all, to see the truth of this.*

On the day of our wedding the little church seemed to be filled with Laurent's ex-girlfriends. One of them was wearing a lovely tangerine chiffon dress and, as the dark trian-

* These differences, of course, do not apply if we are talking about Catholic minorities within Protestant societies. Besieged from the outside, minorities operate under their own laws, making English Catholics an entirely different species from their brethren in southern Europe.

gle revealed, no knickers. The girl in question was a very warm management consultant from Quebec with whom I would become friends.

Only my family and closest friends came. Most of my peers were too broke to afford the trip from England and my side of the church was so sparse that it soon filled up with Laurent's guests. My two girlfriends whom I had accompanied to Victoria Station the summer before were both being pursued by one of Laurent's many cousins, who had sneaked into their hotel bedroom the night before the wedding. So far, he had got nowhere, but he had not given up. Watching their reactions, I remembered the combination of shock and admiration that I had felt at Laurent's own brand of persistence.

After the religious ceremony – which was entirely cosmetic; the real marital contract had been signed before the mayor at the village hall – the guests all traipsed through the fields back to the house for the *vin d'honneur*. This is an old custom, still prevalent in the countryside, which involves the whole village coming to toast the bride. For me, it meant kissing seventy Norman farmers four times each. In France, since the wars of religion, the Protestant minorities have greeted each other with the trinity kiss (three times) and the Catholics with either two or four, depending on the region. That part of Normandy being four, I was kissed that day at least 280 times.

After the *vin d'honneur*, I went and sat down with a group of Laurent's friends from Paris. They were *les Juifs Tun*:

Sephardic Jews whose parents had fled to France from Tunisia after independence. It had not taken me long to notice that these people were different from Laurent's other friends. They threw good parties with decent music, liked a laugh (though not, I had noticed, a drink) and did not care what other people thought of them. These traits made them better company than the manicured bourgeoisie with which Laurent mostly surrounded himself.

Over the past year, I had become close to one woman from this group, a lawyer called Nini who had taken me under her wing from the moment I had arrived, invited me out to lunch, lent me books and gossiped freely with me about everyone in *la bande* – the gang that Laurent had hung around with since his school days. Nini was not only good company; she had a mind like a steel trap and was one of those elaborately perceptive people who made you feel clever just listening to her. It was on the subject of *les Juifs Tun* that Laurent and I had had one of our most vehement rows.

A couple of months before the wedding, Laurent had taken me to a dinner party, during which I had been stunned by a conversation initiated by Nathalie, a pivotal member of Laurent's *bande*. Nathalie's strategy for overcoming the stigma of being ugly in a culture ruthlessly attached to appearances was to visit upon the world a bitterness that most people mistook for wit. Enquiring about the guest list for our wedding, she had discovered that Laurent, with my encouragement, had invited Nini, her two sisters and two of their cousins.

'You'll have to lay on a separate table for them,' she said. 'We won't be able to hear ourselves think otherwise.'

The conversation that followed took on the tone of the habitual racist: a kind of we-all-know-how-we-feel-we-don't-need-to-spell-it-out kind of tone, which amounted to a thinly veiled allusion to the vulgarity and loudness of the *Juif Tun*.

In the car on the way home I called his friends a bunch of anti-Semites.

'They're not anti-Semites. You don't know what you're talking about. They love Nini. They've known her since we were all teenagers.'

'That doesn't stop them from being anti-Semites.'

Although Laurent is not anti-Semitic, he has never understood my argument. His take on the subject was typically French. He refused to accept the idea that making generalisations about a traditionally persecuted minority is a dangerous habit. Nor did he accept that the Jews, by virtue of their history and their status as a minority, should ever be discussed as a category apart. He expected me to accept the notion that if there is no anti-Semitic *intention* behind a remark, then the remark is not anti-Semitic. My proposal that he and his friends were no less anti-Semitic for not being aware of it was absurd to him. It is typically French to believe that so long as you accept the *idea* that all men are equal then they will be, no matter how you treat them.

This state of denial about the reality of racism is very common in France. I have often wondered if it is the result of the nightmare of collaboration, a trauma that is still poorly processed, even today. But then I realise that this same attitude is invariably held with regard to France's Muslim minorities. With its obsession for the founding myth of equality, the French Republic simply cannot accept the concept of the minority group.

So much so that there was an outcry of disgust when the presidential candidate, Nicolas Sarkozy, came out in favour of affirmative action in order to tackle the problem of mass unemployment among French blacks and Muslims. Like any social evolution that goes against the republican model, positive discrimination is beginning to happen on the ground in spite of political resistance to the idea. When a study revealed that a job-seeker with an Arab name has five times less chance of being given an interview in France than someone with a European-sounding name, corporations like Peugeot began to apply the principles of affirmative action in their recruitment programmes, and with some success. Still, the idea of approving this policy nationwide remains taboo.

The French tend to cling firmly to the belief that their country is and always has been an egalitarian meritocracy and that she should not follow the example of Anglo-Saxon societies by talking down to her immigrants and belittling them with quota systems. They see what they refer to as the 'communitarist' model prevalent in Britain and America – where new immigrants settle into communities in which they feel free to preserve their customs and integrate at their own pace – as the ultimate hypocrisy.

The French consider this to be a means devised by the British and American governments of keeping their immigrant populations in poverty and at arm's length. It is not seen as a pragmatic approach to the reality of cultural heterogeneity.

My first encounters with French anti-Semitism came as a shock to me. It was something that my own upbringing had not prepared me for. My generation saw the birth of Channel Four and the quiet revolution of political correctness bring with them the belief that certain opinions were morally unacceptable and needed to be stamped out.

The attitudes I was encountering were clearly a form of low-level cultural anti-Semitism, close to the kind that I had sometimes detected among my parents' generation, and which made otherwise intelligent people like my mother-in-law capable of the most absurd generalisations: 'The Jews are an immensely gifted people, of superior intelligence and they like to stick together.'

For a number of obscure, though historically entrenched reasons, these people also identify these 'gifted' Jews as belonging to a culture that champions money and profit. They are also viewed as being in bed with the Americans in their attachment to values that are deemed to be quintessentially un-French or, as the Vichy regime once put it, *anti-France*. I am convinced that this antipathy is built upon the solid bedrock of Catholic anti-Judaist theology, which right up until Vatican II held the Jews responsible for the death of Christ. What is certain is that French anti-Semitism is inextricable from the deeply rooted distaste for capitalism that was inherited from Catholicism. Today it is often hidden behind or paired with the more acceptable hatred of America.

To me, Nini's uncomplicated attitude towards money marked a welcome change from the feigned parsimony of the rest of Laurent's *bande*. Nini's gang was well off but, unlike their Goyim counterparts, did not bother to hide it. This lack of shame about their fortunes – many of which were built up over decades after having lost everything in Tunisia – was seen by people like Nathalie as vulgar. Behind this view lies the belief, inherited from Catholicism, that profit and gain are sinful. As Nini pointed out to me when we discussed the matter, the Jews are, in theological terms, closer to the Protestants when it comes to attitudes towards money. Calvinism, like Judaism, tends to see material success not as a source of guilt but as a sign of God's favour. For the Catholic Church, profit has long been acquainted with sin. This fact alone explains why Marxism gained such a strong foothold in France, while in the Protestant cultures of Europe it has always remained on the fringes of political life.

France's Catholic heritage has done lasting damage to the reputation of money. Napoleon's scornful judgement of England as 'a nation of shopkeepers' captures the widespread objection to our culture. Georges Pompidou, in a rare outburst of anger, told his friend and colleague Alain Peyrefitte that he was fed up with the French comparing themselves unfavourably with the British. 'We're not like them,' he said. 'If we were we'd know about it! For nearly three centuries we've been idealising Anglo-Saxon society, starting with Montesquieu, who allowed himself to be manipulated by the Intelligence Service . . . This society that we worship is one of Money.'

When I first arrived in France, the nation's long love affair with Marxism was beginning to die, but it was still a political force to be reckoned with. Most of Paris's near suburbs, known as the *ceinture rouge* (red belt), were still run by communist mayors. In the general elections of 1981, the communist candidate, Georges Marchais, had won just over 15 per cent of the vote in the first round, calling on his electorate to support Mitterrand in the second round. Consequently, Mitterrand was honour-bound to invite the PCF (*Parti Communiste Français*) to form a government, and for the first time since 1947, France had (four) communist ministers.

By 1985 the PCF had become a bit of an embarrassment to Mitterrand. Its stubborn refusal to condemn the Russian invasion of Afghanistan and its support for General Jaruzelski's crackdown on the Polish Solidarity movement in 1983 had led to another wave of desertions from the party. As subsequent elections showed, many communists defected to Jean-Marie Le Pen's extreme-right National Front, which, bafflingly, continued to grow. In the European elections of 1984, the National Front won almost 11 per cent of the vote, while the PCF saw its support, compared to the previous elections of 1979, cut in half.

In a particularly cynical piece of political manoeuvring, for which he has been widely criticised, Mitterrand decided to re-establish proportional representation in time for the 1986 general elections. This electoral system was the only one that would enable small parties like the National Front to win any seats in parliament. Thanks to proportional representation, Jean-Marie Le Pen's party won thirty-five seats. By turning the National Front into a legitimate political force for the first time, Mitterrand had split the newly elected right between those willing to form an alliance with the National Front and those who were appalled by the idea. In the same smooth motion, Mitterrand had also delivered a fatal blow to his former ally the PCF, which won the same number of seats as the National Front and whose electorate has declined steadily ever since.

The genetic racism of political extremists like Jean-Marie Le Pen seems, on the surface, a far cry from the anti-materialist and, by extension, anti-capitalist strain in French society. But it is precisely this current that votes for him again and again – often in shame – in election after election. It also explains the strange defection, throughout the eighties, of so many communist voters to the National Front.

Shortly after I arrived in France, this avuncular, glass-eyed veteran from the Franco-Algerian War appeared on national television and called the Holocaust 'a detail' of the Second World War. I was stunned by the fact that he was still being given airtime.

'You can't muzzle him,' Laurent said.

'Why on earth not?'

'Because in some places he wins 30 per cent of the vote.'

Beyond the unifying principle of anti-capitalism, the Le Pen voter is someone who does not feel represented by the governing elite. *Lepenistes* feel themselves to be outside the confines of bourgeois consensus politics – broadly reflected in the dirgeful editorials of *Le Monde* and *Le Figaro*. They believe that voting Le Pen is a means of manifesting their frustration in the face of a political class that bears no resemblance to them. These voters are a rag-tag bunch that certainly includes racists and anti-Semites, but also the ideological heirs to those who fought against the Revolution, people who simply do not identify with the republican dream and who believe that a vote for Le Pen is their only means of dissent. The political genius of Nicolas Sarkozy was to convince these very people that he, and not Le Pen, was the true iconoclast. For the first time since the war, this hitherto silent minority felt they could vote against the system without giving their vote to a fascist.

As I would later discover, when my own offspring turned three and went to nursery school, the republican dream, with all its prejudices and its desires, is implanted early into the hearts and minds of France's children. Expressed in the very language of the teacher and *Monsieur le Directeur* when they welcomed me, as a parent, into *la communauté scolaire* and embedded in the things they chose to teach my children was a morality inherited from the values of the Revolution. This morality – conveyed through words like *solidarité*, *collectivité* and *laïcité* – was generally reasonable, but rarely inspiring. It excluded all those who were attached to values like cultural diversity, spirituality or, in my case, originality and freethinking.

My sister Irene, who also raised her children in France, saw the moral formatting that my children were being exposed to and vowed to make sure it didn't happen to hers. She eschewed a free education and put them into a Steiner school outside Paris. It is a measure of the general climate of mistrust towards any ethos that might conflict with republican values that France's few Steiner schools were at one point put on a list of cult organisations to be watched by the *Renseignements Généraux*.

Language, Yoghurt and Hot Rabbits

My bucolic, shotgun wedding (I was five months pregnant) would be marked with a certain Madame Bovary-like melancholia, helped on by the leaden Normandy skies and my hormonal disarray. The kindness of Laurent's family seemed only to exacerbate my tearfulness. As everybody sat down to lunch, the asphalt clouds opened and the rain beat down on the marquee. The guests sat through the long, muggy afternoon, waiting for the party to begin. My brother-in-law had kindly offered to be the

DJ, and I had been to enough French parties to dread the results. My pregnancy meant that I was more than usually emotional, and as I stood at the edge of the tent and watched my new husband moving among the guests, I felt a wave of alienation. I looked at the small huddle of friends from England. The men – or, more accurately, boys – were all wearing dark suits and sunglasses, like extras from *The Blues Brothers*; they were all clutching their drinks and, I guessed, feeling baffled and a little depressed by the sobriety of the occasion. As I looked at my dashing, juvenile father-in-law flirting with one of my closest friends; at my handsome, long-suffering mother-in-law floating about in her silk sari; at Aurélie, the should-have-been-me sex goddess – also dressed in white – and at my new husband, presiding over a table of earnest smokers, deep in what I knew would be 'intellectual conversation', I was seized by an overwhelming desire to run away, back to my unsophisticated student life, back home to England.

Instead, I went and sat down beside Laurent and hovered on the edge of the conversation, a position I was finding increasingly uncomfortable but from which it would take me about five years to disengage. Living in France and not speaking French properly is a torturous business that cannot be compared to the experience of living in England with approximate English or in Spain with bad Spanish. The French are, as it has often been noted, ruthlessly unforgiving of foreigners. The reason for this is that they love their language beyond all reason. ('My country', as Albert Camus put it, 'is the French language.') They relish it, turn it in their mouths and savour it like wine in a way that smacks of the obscene to most Brits, for whom language is principally a means to an end. French is not an efficient language. There are too few nouns for it to be properly useful. It is a language given to digression and subordinate clauses – the language of diplomacy, the language of non-commitment. It would take many years for me to be able to enjoy it for this very reason: in French you can be as long-winded and pretentious as you like. No one will blame you for it. In fact, the sight of a foreigner who appears to be enjoying their language is a pleasurable experience for French people – like watching a person really savour something you've cooked for them.

There is, on the other hand, no tolerance for the learning process. The French do not like to hear their language spoken badly. They would rather butcher yours than hear theirs being eviscerated: hence their very rude tendency to reply in bad English after you've been struggling in French. I believe that the reason for this intolerance is that language is central to their culture in a way that it is not in Britain. The French are addicted to ideas, and their language, with all its wonderful imprecision, is a perfect vehicle for abstraction.

The British are, by contrast, rooted in the concrete. Their talent for comic detachment enables them to communicate in ways that are not necessarily linked to the expression of ideas. Indeed they mistrust ideas, which are seen as the domain of the pretentious. A sense of the absurd or a sense of irony will be enough to make someone entertaining in Britain, whereas both these faculties are frequently lost on the French.

This love of ideas explains the status of the intellectual in French culture. In Britain we have journalists, social commentators, academics, but we don't have *les intellectuels* – those foppish, self-regarding creatures who clog the French media and regularly hit the best-seller lists with titles like *The Meaning of Beauty* or *The Misery of Prosperity*, which many people buy, everyone discusses, but rather fewer actually read. A figure like Bernard-Henri Levy has only recently become an object of derision in France. For years he was her most glamorous and sought-after intellectual. With his handsome face, mane of dark hair and trademark white shirt unbuttoned to reveal an eternally juvenile chest, he has been wheeled out for decades to comment on every social ripple from fashion to war. Having achieved international notoriety by his posturing on the geopolitical stage – first in Sarajevo, then in Afghanistan – he became every Paris correspondent's favourite interview (apart from Le Pen and, more recently, Carla Bruni). Since becoming the object of Anglo-Saxon derision, however, even his French public now see how ridiculous he is. I, personally, have always been intrigued by his shameless narcissism. I once followed him for about twenty minutes down the Boulevard Saint-Germain and was astounded by the frequency with which he checked his reflection in the shop windows.

In Britain, communication can exist beyond and in spite of language in a way that it cannot in France. The miraculously bonding effect of alcohol, for example, operates in British culture beyond language, so that it is enough to have a few pints and watch some sport together in order to determine whether someone's company is good or bad. In France, this judgement can only be made according to a person's capacity to express and exchange ideas. There is also – and this is true of every milieu – a deep love of loud debate. To say of a conversation that it is *Café du Commerce* refers to the widespread practice of sitting around and talking loudly, though not necessarily informedly, about one's ideas. This love of ideas has dominated the history of France, conditioned her particular brand of colonialism and led her to Glory or Ignominy, depending on your perspective. Napoleon said, 'There is no occupation more honourable, or more useful to nations, than to contribute to the extension of human ideas. The real power of the French Republic must henceforth lie in the assurance that no new idea exists that is not hers.'*

Napoleon also said that the essence of France is the French language well written. Because of their logocentric culture, the French like their politicians to be eloquent. One of the main objections formulated by her opponents against the candidate Ségolène Royal was that she spoke badly. For an entire week in the run-up to the last presi-

* Napoleon Bonaparte, 'Lettre à l'Institut après son éléction le 25 décembre 1797', published by *Le Moniteur*.

dential elections, the media was dominated by her use of the word *bravitude* for 'bravery' (a neologism of her own invention). Following in the footsteps of her mentor, François Mitterrand, Royal was standing on the Great Wall of China with an escort from the Chinese Communist Party when she made the linguistic *faux pas*. The word she should have used was *bravoure*. Her opponents seized on the slip as the ultimate proof of her unsuitability as president, whose French, it was pointed out, had to be 'pure and irreproachable'.

For Royal's supporters, the gaps in her education were a sign of 'authenticity'. Indeed, her sudden rise to stardom before the presidential race was in part the result of a growing backlash against the kind of eloquence that was being seen increasingly as a trademark of the ruling classes, trained in the art of rhetoric by the same prestigious schools, ENA (Ecole Nationale d'Administration) and Polytechnique. Her opponent, Nicolas Sarkozy, rarely missed the opportunity of pointing out that, unlike her, he had attended neither of these schools but had trained as a lawyer. He also claimed to have a mistrust of ideas, unprecedented in a French politician. In the introduction to his extremely popular autobiography, *Témoignage*, Sarkozy wrote, 'In my opinion words, ideas, communication, only mean something if they permit, but more importantly, facilitate action.' These words sound like common sense in English. In French, they are highly polemical.

With the exception of de Gaulle, whose extensive oeuvre related entirely to defence and military matters, a widely proclaimed love of literature and art has always been a necessary part of the presidential profile in France. Georges Pompidou – the man behind Rogers and Piano's iconoclastic Pompidou Centre and one of the key initiators of France's lavish and robust cultural policy – edited an anthology of French poetry that is still in print. His successor, Valérie Giscard d'Estaing (in spite of the fact that he has only published one, rather mediocre novel called *Le Passage*), has the reputation of a man of letters and was elected to France's most illustrious literary body, *L'Académie Française*. Even Chirac, with his badly cut suits and his dubious reputation for preferring beer to wine, writes rhyming poetry and is adept in the art of Alexandrine verse, a talent that he has used to seduce more than one mistress. Mitterrand, probably the most intellectual of all the presidents of the Fifth Republic, published nine books during his lifetime, two of which were collaborations – one with the Nobel Prize winner Elie Wiesel and the other with the novelist Marguerite Duras.

It appears that the more overtly literary France's politicians are the more promiscuous they seem to be. François Mitterrand, throughout his open marriage to Danielle, has been described as a bumble bee, constructing his parallel love lives like a complex honeycomb. Beyond the tranquil haven of his 'secret life' with Anne Pingeot and Mazarine and the duties of his marriage to Danielle, the Elysée Palace became a hub of erotic activity. It has been said of him that he tried, and invariably succeeded, in seducing any attractive woman who passed through his office. An employee from those heady days explained how one summer the president hired a helicopter to meet one of his new conquests. Another civil servant recounts how, on a state visit to Switzerland, the president decided, after breakfast and in the middle of his official programme, to look up one of his old flames: 'We waited on the doorstep . . . At the appointed time we knocked on the door and the official schedule continued.'

Sex and power are seen in France as intertwined; or, as Henry Kissinger put it, 'Power is the ultimate aphrodisiac.' But while the American public will ultimately punish their politicians for libidinousness, the French will always admire and applaud them. Chirac is known as 'Monsieur ten minutes, shower included,' and viewed affectionately – even by those who would never vote for him – as a *bon vivant*, a man with a Rabelaisian appetite for life.

In this frivolous nation, the career of any politician (male or female) who does not appear to be interested in the art of seduction will suffer as a result. The dark years of the Nazi Occupation no doubt made the prudish figure of General de Gaulle an exception to this rule. But men of moral rectitude, like Edouard Balladur or Lionel Jospin, even Michel Rocard (who suffered a lapse in rigour late in life by having an affair and then, like the Protestant that he is, leaving his wife), are broadly perceived as unsexy. Indeed, all three of these politicians were thwarted by voters when within sight of the presidency. When I asked Laurent about this puzzling state of affairs, he taught me a new expression.

'Politicians have to be *chauds lapins*,' he said. 'The more they seem to enjoy sex, the more it adds to their charisma.'

Hot Rabbits?

That rainy afternoon of my wedding, I watched the earnest gesticulation, the heavy drawing on cigarettes, the trappings of intense debate, and felt bored and stupid. I couldn't have guessed that in years to come I too would develop a taste for abstract conversation that would make my English friends squirm with embarrassment.

It has often been observed that the habit of embarrassment is quintessentially English. That night, when my brother-in-law began to play a rotation of Queen, Pink Floyd, Supertramp and his collection of rousing French hits from the seventies and eighties, the party divided into those who were embarrassed and those who were not. The French flooded onto the dance floor and began to jive expertly or else jump up and down and sing along at the tops of their voices, while the English huddled together in the hope that they might achieve invisibility.

That was the first time I heard the expression *yaourt*.

'Yoghurt' is the word used to describe the practice of singing along to tracks in English, usually with an unconvincing American accent, when you have absolutely no idea of the words. Yoghurt doesn't have to *be* English, it only has to *sound* English. Singing along to 'I Want to Break Free' in Yoghurt would sound something like this: 'I wo' do' bek fee.' Sit on the Metro and you'll hear plenty of amateur French R'n'B singers doing 'Papa gode a ban noo bang' in perfect Yoghurt. There are even current French expressions derived from Yoghurt. My favourite is '*C'est la waneugaine*' – a bizarre distortion of the English, *once again* – meaning it's crazy or outlandish.

With a few notable exceptions, French pop music is by and large diabolical. Often described as the art form that calls least upon the intellect, music relies too much on intuition and the imagination to be really accessible to the French, who are coached from birth for rational thought. Ballads are fine, because they are firmly rooted in an easy melodic tradition and there are plenty of words: hence the particular genius of a composer like Serge Gainsbourg. There is no need, however, for any musical excellence in the rendition of these songs, so long as the singer *looks* good. That is why the French are quite happy to listen to some tone-deaf actress with a breathy voice, like Adjani or Deneuve or Bardot, sing Gainsbourg's compositions. It also explains why Serge Gainsbourg's ex-wife, Jane Birkin – a pretty, sixty-year-old *femme-enfant* with no voice – is an icon of the music business here and why her concerts are always sold out.

For a nation with such little aptitude for music, the French are wonderfully enthusiastic about it. In the early years of François Mitterrand's presidency, just before he made his spectacular U-turn in economic policy, France was in the deepest doldrums. Those who had voted for him were bitterly disappointed that his bold decision to invite the communists into his cabinet, followed by his audacious programme of nationalisations, appeared not to have worked; nor had raising the minimum wage, shortening the working week and lengthening the annual paid holiday improved the quality of their lives. (Mass unemployment, the collapse of the French stock market and a global recession certainly didn't help.) Those who had not voted for Mitterrand were appalled that they were living in an almost Soviet-style economy in which the state had a 95 per cent share in banking and one in four people was working for the public sector. By June 1982, under pressure from his finance minister, Jacques Delors, Mitterrand made several currency devaluations and introduced a series of austerity measures, suddenly making himself the most unpopular president since the founding of the Fifth Republic. In the midst of this misery and hardship, Mitterrand's popular, perma-tanned culture minister, Jack Lang, pulled an old idea out of the drawer and the *Fête de la Musique* was born.

This, as I soon discovered, is an annual celebration of French musical mediocrity during which all manner of amateur musicians are invited to come out onto the streets of their city, town or village and 'Make Music!' (*Faites de la Musique!*). In the tradition of popular festivals dear to the French Republic in its quest to provide meaning to a society that is at once rigorously secular and prone to idealism, Jack Lang chose the summer solstice, 21 June, for his music day. Every year since 1982, the French have celebrated the arrival of summer and on that night 'Yoghurt' fills the streets. The first time Laurent and I went together to the *Fête de la Musique* would, I swore at the time, be the last. Lone, middle-aged electric guitarists, long thwarted in their ambitions, had come out of their basements to stand on street corners and play that Led Zeppelin riff over and over again, while rapturous teenagers banged their heads in appreciation. The culture ministry had not shown our eighteenth arrondissement the bounty she had shown other parts of the city, and there were no professional concerts that night, only the keen cacophony of amateur musicians, with their bongos, their accordions or their keyboards, playing cover versions on café terraces while everybody – young and old – danced together.

In spite of my vow never to go again, I would, with time, be infected by this French gift for innocent ebullience and take my children to the *Fête de la Musique*. Most years it would rain and we would wander through the warm, wet streets of Paris, slipping in our flip-flops as we danced with strangers to the terrible music. At the risk of sounding priggish, there is no need for money, or drugs, or alcohol, to have a good time at the *Fête de la Musique*, nor is there anything to fear from letting your children wander the streets until dawn. French self-restraint, which is so often a bore, in circumstances like these becomes a blessing. The equivalent to the *Fête de la Musique* could not exist in Britain. Not only would the music have to be of a higher standard – thereby destroying the rather makeshift, spontaneous flavour – but also the event would have to be accompanied by huge quantities of drugs and alcohol and a considerable police presence. Good, clean fun is not feasible in today's Britain.

One of the advantages of France's rather undistinguished musical status (despite more recent aberrations like Air, Daft Punk, Justice or Kid Loco) is that the French have not been affected by the tyranny of Cool. The vast majority of French people are not ashamed of looking ridiculous while dancing to bad pop music, and I find this very charming. When my father-in-law pulled me onto the dance floor on the evening of my wedding and piloted me expertly through a jive, I wished that the ground would swallow me up. Having lived for so long in a country where people suffer so little from embarrassment, I can now appreciate how liberating is the experience of being completely uncool. Later, while the guests swayed in unison to 'A Kind of Magic', Laurent and I drove off on our honeymoon.

6 Sublime, Necessarily Sublime

Mayors, Mass Demonstration and Mayhem

We spent a lazy and idyllic honeymoon in a house in Provence belonging to one of Laurent's aunts. It was a pretty stone bungalow, overgrown with lavender and rosemary, on the edge of a sleepy, unspoilt village in Vaucluse called Puyméras. The village has since expanded and many of the surrounding vineyards have been swept away to make room for the new, uniformly pastel, mock-Provençal houses that now litter the hillsides. Anyone who has any experience of real estate in rural France will know all about the arbitrary and absolute power of the village mayor.

It was Mitterrand and his minister Gaston Deferre, back in the early days of his mandate, who, in an attempt to decentralise the French State, bolstered the power of little dictators to make or break village life in France. Despite a steady rural exodus since the mid-sixties which has resulted in the majority of the population now living in towns, the fabric of French society is still an intricate patchwork of small villages. Three-quarters of her thirty-six thousand communes are made up of villages of less than a thousand inhabitants, over whom *Monsieur* or *Madame le Maire* may reign supreme.

Since the early eighties most of these villages have been disfigured by anarchic building on their outskirts. Anarchic is perhaps the wrong word for these *lotissements*, as they're called, for they tend to be uniform in their architectural conception, each region possessing its own template, its own parody of the vernacular. In Provence, all new constructions must be covered in a sickly salmon render to echo the sun-kissed limestone of old, and in the French Basque Country they must have mock wattle-and-daub façades with ox-blood shutters.

The steady selling-off of lots surrounding France's villages has been a prized source of revenue for some of the many small-holding farmers, *paysans*, who have gradually lost their livelihoods over the past three decades. This practice has profited all those lucky enough to own land close to villages like Puyméras, as well as, in some cases, the mayors who delivered the building permits. It has also been a short-term gain that has threatened the future of thousands of communities, which have overbuilt on their most fertile land, polluted their water tables and created unsustainable communities no longer in a position to develop the kind of specialised or ecological agriculture that could save them.

In those days Puyméras was still pretty idyllic. There was a vibrant café owned by a man who went by the decorous name of 'Zizi' (French children's word for penis), who offered barbecued *merguez* sausages and live music on Saturday nights. The band consisted of a young man who did Yoghurt versions of Michael Jackson hits, complete with pelvic dance moves and accompanied by a woman on a synthesiser. Already I was finding it easier to dance along happily with the rest of the village to 'A gonna be starvin' sunshine'.

It was on the drive home to Paris that I first understood the significance of the *congé payé*, the French tradition of the one-month paid holiday. It was 15 August and the Catholic festival of the Assumption of the Virgin Mary. The roads were packed with families beginning or ending their holidays. In spite of the terrible traffic, the atmosphere was one of joy and camaraderie. Families were putting out aluminium chairs and tables and inviting each other to lunch in lay-bys or even right there, where they had halted, by the side of the *autoroute*. The *congé payé* is a privilege or, as the French call it, an *acquis social* which, broadly speaking, refers to any right which has been won through social or industrial action and which no one is prepared to give up without a fight. French politicians are notoriously wary of tampering with anything that can be described as an *acquis social*, for they know that it will unleash the terrifying, debilitating power of the mass demonstration.

The *congé payé* dates back to the Popular Front, the socialist coalition presided over by France's first Jewish prime minister, Léon Blum. The *Front Populaire* was carried to power in 1936 on a wave of anti-fascism, and its short, two-year mandate is still perceived as the Glory Days of French socialism. As well as introducing the forty-hour working week, Blum introduced the *congé payé*, which would make the month of August a virtually compulsory paid holiday for the entire adult working population of France. Even today, everyone is legally entitled to five weeks off a year and many decide, however inconvenient for business, to take most of it in one balmy chunk. Even committed capitalists put up the shutters in August as their suppliers are rarely available for business.

This mass exodus from working life creates a very particular atmosphere, especially in the vacated towns. The mood in Paris in August is entirely different from the rest of the year. Given over to the mercy of happy, badly dressed tourists, the city becomes gentler, freer, less imperious. Kids from the suburbs, somehow kept at bay by the Parisians for the rest of the year, feel permitted to spill over onto her elegant streets on August nights; the footbridges are alive with bad bongo players, amateur jugglers and other unabashedly uncool samples of French youth. Those Parisians who do stay behind in August revel in the *luxe calme et volupté* of the slacking city, and the place becomes more erotically charged than ever. I recently learnt of the existence of August brothels. Open Monday to Friday from 1 to 31 August, they cater specifically to husbands whose wives and children have left for the country or the seaside. These husbands stay and work in Paris in the week and then take the train to join their families on Friday nights. To even things out, the Friday-night trains are called *Les Trains des Cocus* (the cuckolds' trains), packed as they are with men whose wives have been having it away all week with their children's tennis instructors.

In August Paris drops her guard and people gain direct access to each other. The city is a coded, trussed-up place most of the year, but in August people talk to each other in bus queues. The only other time one experiences camaraderie like this in Paris is during periods of mass demonstration. It is widely acknowledged as a harsh reality of political life in this country that it is the street that dictates reform. Or rather, it is the street that paralyses reform. Indeed, Laurent explained his own paradoxical politics to me in the following terms: 'If you want anything to change in France, you have to vote socialist because only the socialists are able to push through reforms.'

This contrary position made no sense to me at the time, but it soon became clear that while Mitterrand was president, the street allowed his socialist government more room to manoeuvre than it would the Chirac government when it finally came to power in 1986. That winter was dominated by mass student demonstrations, which put an end to an educational reform that had been called for by politicians on both left and right for years. The Devaquet Project was an attempt to allow universities more independence from central government in determining fees and selection procedures. On Thursday 27 November two hundred thousand students took to the streets of Paris. Nine days later, as the demonstrations were still in full swing, twenty-two-year-old Malik Oussekine, an innocent bystander on his way out of a jazz club, was chased by a group of motorcycle cops marshalling the demonstrators and beaten up in the lobby of an apartment building. He died in hospital from his injuries. In the wake of his death, the education minister resigned and Chirac withdrew the reform. He is convinced to this day that it was his capitulation that led to his defeat in the subsequent presidential elections of 1988. He has been said to have sworn never again to give in to pressure from the street. Indeed, his solution to this problem seems to have been to avoid any confrontation at all, his presidential style having been characterised by a stasis and inaction rarely seen in history.

During the nineties France's right-wing governments withdrew every single significant reform after mass demonstrations. Prime Minister Edouard Balladur abandoned both his labour and his education reforms, as did Prime Minister Alain Juppé in his attempts to reform the pension and social security systems. In November and December 1995, a general strike was called to combat the *Plan Juppé*. It mobilised workers from the railway services, post office, telephone and electricity services, Social Security, hospital and education, the emergency services, local government, airports, transport workers and miners. Joined by the student population, the country ground to a halt.

The effectiveness of public demonstrations in this country came as a surprise to me. I had been a teenager under

Margaret Thatcher. My first demonstrations had been in support of the miners' strike and against public spending cuts, and I had become resigned to the fatuousness of marching. Indeed, in Britain it seemed that demonstrations only did damage to a cause. In Paris, some group or other was marching every week, and the deputies in the Assembly were, for good or ill, taking their demands into consideration.

There was an atmosphere of collective jubilation during that winter of 1995. Parisians from all walks of life banded together. No matter what their feelings about the reforms themselves, they gave each other lifts in their cars and cheered on the chaos. Civil unrest on a scale like this seemed to bring out the milk of human kindness in these people, generally known for their sullenness. This spirit, this uniting against authority, is encapsulated in the French word *solidarité*, a word that has a magic ring to it. Mitterrand's prime minister Michel Rocard used it to soften the blow when he renamed the new supertax from *Impôt sur la Grande Fortune* to *Impôt de Solidarité sur la Fortune* (ISF). France's equivalent of the civil partnership, voted in after much debate in 1999, was named the *Pacte Civil de Solidarité* (Civil Pact of Solidarity). The word *solidarity* is important. It upholds the myth of France as a caring society and enables the individual to go on pursuing his or her interests with a clear conscience.

French people adhere to the idea of solidarity because they know that at one time or another they're going to need it in order to defend their interests in a society made up of a myriad of concessions and privileges that have been grappled from the clutches of that monolithic arbiter of all things, the State.

Nobility, Freedom and Status

Once back in Paris, Laurent and I settled into married life. In September the city always returns to her natural posture of hostility and mistrust. I spent a good deal of my time crying in the face of daily expressions of scorn from strangers, and Laurent spent much of his trying to repair the damage. Today, my vulnerability in the face of dismissive shop girls, truculent civil servants and rude waiters seems a little pathetic to me. But at the time the rudeness of strangers devastated me. Pregnancy hormones, I'm sure, didn't help, but when I look back at how I behaved in the face of these assaults, I realise that I was simply ill-equipped. All the social skills I had acquired growing up in Britain did me no good at all. My politeness, the constant pleases and thank yous, the self-deprecating posture – all of it only made me more of a target for people's contempt.

'You don't have to be so *apologetic*,' Laurent would whisper to me after I had ordered in a restaurant. 'There's no shame in the fact that he's serving you.'

Of course he was right. The waiter interpreted my sycophancy as a mark of disrespect for his trade. Laurent explained that in France being a waiter was a noble profession. Waiters were not out-of-work actors or writers or people hoping for something better to come along.

Brasserie and restaurant waiters, in particular, have often fought for their positions, sometimes even paid for them, and many keep their jobs for life.

All this explained Laurent's rather curt restaurant manner. He would state his order simply and clearly, without ceremony or apology, without a please or thank you, often without looking up so as not to engage personally. That way it became the waiter's prerogative to initiate contact. He could be perfectly anonymous if he felt like it or he could make some witty remark to which Laurent would respond with an appreciative chuckle. This way, client and waiter were on an equal footing. There was no master–servant guilt.

France is a nation that is at once obsessed with the idea of nobility and the idea of equality. This paradox at the heart of her mythology explains the particular explosiveness of her society. The solution to this paradox, offered first by the monarchy and picked up by the Republic, seems to lie in the word 'status'. Everyone in France has a *statut*, which is probably best translated by the military word *rank*. Waiters have a specific *statut*, just as the *boulanger* has his (or hers), as does the railway worker, the teacher, the painter, the plumber . . . Each profession forms part of a *corps* (another military word) *de métier*. The *corps de métier* is a clear echo of the medieval guild. Members of the medieval French guilds were bound to their lord and master for life. With each guild came a *statut* and with it a set of privileges; it was often these privileges that made the job bearable. This idea of a job coming with its particular status and set of privileges endures today, even when economic realities have swept many of the privileges away. The fact that the French do not see much glory in productivity or even money goes a long way towards explaining their stubborn refusal to relinquish the few remaining privileges – early retirement, free train travel or long holidays – that are linked to their particular profession.

In France the idea of personal freedom is inextricably linked to the idea of Nobility. The Revolution's slogan – *Liberté, Egalité, Fraternité* . . . or Death (a coda rarely remembered) – places freedom as the highest value. What is rarely admitted is that the Revolution's particular idea of freedom is deeply indebted to the values of the *Ancien Régime*. Indeed, it is as if the patrician values of the French monarchy were, by miraculous sleight of hand, incorporated into those of the Revolution. Bizarrely, for the French, even the post-revolutionary French, the idea of freedom is embodied in the life of the nobleman. To this day it is the obsolete aristocrat who remains the ideal model of a free man; free to rise above the drudgery of everyday, material concerns in order that he or she may delight in the life of the mind. Indeed, it is part of the function of the State to preserve and enable this very dream.

The French idea of freedom could hardly be more different from the Anglo-Saxon notion. Set out most clearly in the philosophy of the seventeenth-century English philosopher John Locke, and even echoed, a century later, by the conservative thinker Edmund Burke, the English notion of freedom which would be inherited by America's founding fathers is inseparable from the idea of *property*. For both the liberal Locke and the conservative Burke, freedom can be defined by the pragmatic observation that one man's freedom ends where another man's begins, and that means with the boundaries of his property. In England, as in America, a man is free as long as his person and his property remain inviolable. His freedom is guaranteed by the law from any arbitrary intervention, be it from the State or an individual: 'Man hath by nature a power to preserve his property, that is, his Life, Liberty and Estate, against the Injuries and Attempts of other Men.' In America, the right to bear arms has forever been entangled with this fundamental right to the defence of one's property.

The French Revolution, of course, made a mockery of this belief by confiscating the property of Church and aristocracy. Edmund Burke expressed his outrage at the goings-on in France and his protests reflected the deep conviction that the Englishman's house was his castle: 'You will observe that from Magna Charta to the Declaration of Right it has been the uniform policy of our constitution to claim and assert our liberties as an entailed inheritance derived to us from our forefathers, and to be transmitted to our posterity.'

It is hard to imagine the British monarchy, for instance, ever having managed to convince the aristocracy to abandon their estates and move, complete with servants and livery, to the court. Surely the Versailles experiment and the resulting submission to the will of *Le Roi Soleil* indicates that for the French the idea of Freedom is not linked to the idea of property but to that of nobility. Louis XIV cleverly manipulated this belief and thereby managed to establish an elaborate hierarchy around his person that fully occupied five thousand courtiers.

For the French, on the other hand, equating liberty with the freedom to dispose of one's property is to debase the idea of liberty, which must carry the connotation of nobility or grandeur. To be free of material concerns is one of the principal attributes of true liberty, for the world of commerce induces a form of enslavement: enslavement to profit, to wages, to gain.

In English society, even in feudal times, the idea of freedom was linked to property. There was no such thing as life-time servitude unless, that is, it was voluntarily given. Legally, an English serf's obligation to his Lord ended the moment he returned the goods and property that had been given in exchange for his services. Theoretically, at least, this rudimentary contract was guaranteed by the King's Justice.

In medieval France, on the other hand, the vassal vowed life-time devotion to his Lord, in exchange for which he received the status and privileges that were compatible with the nature of his service. The status conferred respectability and dignity and provided, within the confines of subordination to the honoured lord, a sense of belonging to a community of equals. This paradoxical notion of equality within a hierarchy persists in France today. It can be seen in its purest form within the French Public Service, where employees are so imbued with a sense of nobility that they refuse all modification or reform of their status. As Alexis de Tocqueville said of the French: 'They want equality in freedom but if they can't have that, they'll want it in slavery.'

This heritage goes a long way to explaining the attitudes of people employed in the service of the State. From post office workers to railway clerks to teachers, the French have traditionally been brought up to believe that there is no position more secure, more comfortable, nor more worthy than *Le Service Public*, and they will leap through countless hoops to get there. The endless tests and exams in order to become a civil servant, even at the most junior levels, contribute to the sense of having been 'chosen', and the smug, haughty, intransigent manner of the man or woman behind that sheet of glass is the result of a very particular combination of the pride of belonging to an illustrious caste and a certain resentment about the realities of belonging to that caste.

For as in most aspects of French life, there is a huge gap between the idea and the reality. The reality, of course, is the drudgery of stasis, of the repetitive task and the increasingly problematic confrontation with the outside world, which has its own expectations and demands. On the other side of that counter or window the world is shifting, people are starting to brandish phrases like 'customer service', and the great tide of Anglo-Saxon Protestant capitalism, bringing with it concepts like job flexibility and privatisation, is threatening to sweep away privilege and certainty. The only rampart against this tide is the State itself, and the State has failed.

In France, the civil servant's mentality is not confined to the *Service Public*. It is everywhere. You can encounter it in organisations that are supposed to be committed to the idea of private enterprise. My local bookshop, which is part of a small chain affiliated with the illustrious publishers Gallimard, is one such place. Recently I bought a novel there for a friend, only to discover that she already had it. On my way to have lunch with my son, I took the book back and chose another novel by the same author, which was a little cheaper. Instead of giving me the change, the woman at the cash register offered me an *avoir* (credit note) for two euros fifty. I told her that I would rather have the money, to which she replied that they didn't give out cash. The smugness of her delivery was so irritating that I asked to see the manager. She huffed, and marched to the back of the shop. I could tell from her gesticulations that she expected to be defended by her boss, which of course she was. The manager was a middle-aged man with exactly the same attitude: what I was asking was simply 'not done', he explained. When I dishonestly pointed out that I was a foreigner and would not be likely to ever use my *avoir*, he apologised in the most unapologetic way possible and repeated that it couldn't be done. I asked him why, and he folded his arms and said, 'Because we don't do it, Madame.'

'But what about customer service? Can't you be a bit flexible?'

To which he replied, 'The customer has to respect the rules like everybody else, Madame.'

This was his profound conviction: all equal in slavery. By this time a small queue had gathered behind me and people were watching me with marked hostility. I was making a scene. I was probably American. I had come to their country and tried to impose my free-market mentality on their egalitarian system.

By the time I got to the café where I was meeting my son, I was fuming with rage. This was something that hadn't happened to me for a long time. I usually took this kind of behaviour in my stride, laughed it off, saw it as part of a wider context that brought with it an array of other, wonderful things: long lunches, paid holidays, a pleasant lack of competitiveness . . . Today I had relapsed.

My son, Jack, who was in his first year at the Sorbonne studying philosophy, laughed when I told him the story. He had just read Nietzsche and explained the attitude I had encountered in the following terms: 'Nietzsche said there were two types of mentality in the world, defending two opposing kinds of civilisation: the slave mentality and the noble mentality. The slave mentality basically says "No" to life and the noble mentality says "Yes".'

In Nietzsche's merciless view of humanity, Jack explained, men were born with either a slave's or a nobleman's mentality, the former fuelled by resentment and envy and the latter by the conquering spirit and the will to power. Nietzsche believed that the first champion of the slave mentality was Socrates and among the civilisations built upon it were Christianity and Marxism.

'What you encountered in the bookshop,' Jack explained, 'that habit of saying, "No, it can't be done," is a pure example of what Nietzsche was talking about. Fear of change, devotion to a system, mistrust of the individual will; these are all manifestations of the slave mentality.'

The French paradox, then, lies in the attachment of its population to an apparently noble status that ultimately enslaves them.

It has often been pointed out that Protestant culture is a culture based on 'confidence', confidence in the individual as an autonomous, self-regulating entity. Theoretically, in this type of society, the State believes in the idea of limiting its own role. France, in turning her back on the Reformation, chose to maintain a hierarchical system in which the individual would continue to be both dominated and pampered by the State. The history of France is the history of her people's paradoxical or at least dual relationship with authority. As René Rémond, one of France's leading political scientists, put it: 'The attitude of the French towards authority, throughout history, proceeds from a double and contradictory heritage: the cult of the State and the inclination to rebellion.'*

This oscillation between contestation and worship

* René Rémond, 'La société française et l'autorité', *Ville-Ecole-Intégration* 112 (March 1998).

occurred throughout the *Ancien Regime*, both towards the monarchy and the Catholic hierarchy, anti-clericalism having always been much stronger in the French than in their Catholic neighbours. In a family with a powerful father figure, perceived to be at once tyrannical and indulgent, the children find a kind of reassurance in the perpetual interface with the authority figure; indeed, they are defined by it. So it is with the French and their State.

This legacy, however, is being undermined by an equally powerful current, which is gathering momentum and is generally referred to as 'the Anglo-Saxon model'. Today, political discourse in France is entirely conditioned by where you stand on this influence, whether you are for it or against it, whether it is something to be embraced or resisted at all costs. This ideological divide does not follow party lines. It is also a divide that dares not speak its name.

When Nicolas Sarkozy came along with his defiant mantra on the value of work, he was striking at the very heart of the republican dream. His electoral message was revolutionary because it was quintessentially un-French. 'I propose the following options to the new presidential majority: social policy . . . work, educational policy . . . work, economic policy . . . work, fiscal policy . . . work, commercial policy . . . work, immigration policy . . . work, monetary policy . . . work, budgetary policy . . . work. What I'm proposing is to make our politics the politics of work.'

Apart from during the ignominious Vichy period, work has never been a value in France. Nor, indeed, has profit. The prevailing moral code, inherited from the *Ancien Regime*, sees work and gain as a means to an end; the end being an elevated life. The Catholic Church did not adopt the idea of salvation through work, and post-revolutionary France, in its clever appropriation of Catholic values, knew better than to integrate the work ethic into its new ideology.

During my first winter with Laurent the papers were filled with the chilling story of the murder of a four-year-old child called Gregory. The story – that came to be known as 'Le Petit Gregory' in an eerie echo of Perrault's fairy tale 'Le Petit Poucet' – would grip the French imagination for years to come, and the mystery remains unsolved to this day. But it was not so much the story itself that fascinated me but, like Zidane's head-butt decades later, the particular way in which it was told and interpreted.

For months the prime murder suspect was Gregory's mother, Christine Villemin. Christine's cold beauty seemed to incite extremes of feeling, and the country was divided between those who saw her as a victim and those for whom she was a monster. Nine months after little Gregory's body was found, bound with rope, in the Vologne river that flows through the dark, industrial valleys of the Vosges mountains, an article appeared in *Libération** that seemed to be an attempt to unite this polarised view of Christine.

* 17 July 1985.

The article was written by Marguerite Duras, at the time France's most eminent female writer and winner, that same year, of the Goncourt Prize for her world-famous novel *L'Amant* (*The Lover*). The long piece, marked with Duras's special brand of laconic lyricism, entirely presumed the poor woman's guilt (Villemin would later be acquitted), but went on to 'forgive' her for her supposed crime. Extolling the defendant's will to overcome the narrow circumstances of her life, Duras paints a picture of a working-class Medea who chooses infanticide in a grandiose bid for freedom.

The article, which was published under the dazzling title 'Sublime, Necessarily Sublime', still strikes me today as emblematic of the particular blindness of the Parisian bourgeois intellectual. Embedded in Duras's absurd eulogy are all of France's founding myths and obsessions: the taste for the tragic, the obsession for nobility, grandeur, freedom and equality. For mad though it may sound, Duras suggests in her piece that the subject of her fantasy, Christine Villemin, by killing her own child, somehow rises above her social status: 'I see only her,' says Duras. 'At the centre of the world, surpassed by only time and God.'

7 Maternity

Glory, Breastfeeding and the Norm

When I told my tutors at Oxford that I was pregnant, they kindly granted me a year off. I would have the baby in France and return for my final year. Some of them, I'm sure, thought that I wouldn't come back, but they were all very supportive. In my college, which had only recently started admitting women, this was a first, and the dons seemed determined to be as positive as they could be.

In Paris that winter I was undergoing my gradual transformation. My resistance to the cult of appearances was being worn away, and I found that going out in my bedroom slippers was something I would no longer consider. Every month I went for a check-up at the maternity hospital where I was due to give birth in December. A girlfriend of mine, an anaesthetist called Sandrine, had recommended it to me for its glamorous head of obstetrics, Professor Minkowski, a renowned specialist in neonate and developmental biology.

In France, the best practitioners work in the public sector. The State pays them a standard wage and they are allowed to augment their income with private consultations outside the hospital. When I asked Sandrine why they stayed with the public service, she simply answered: '*Pour la Gloire* [for the glory].'

There is more prestige in the Health Service than out of it. Practitioners are decently paid but, more importantly, they are respected and admired. Within the lavish public health system they can carry out their research, publish their findings and achieve that most prized of French dreams, not wealth or glamour, but that old-fashioned commodity, recognition.

As it turned out, I never clapped eyes on Professor Minkowski. Like most French National Health maternity hospitals, his was run by a team of midwives. He would only appear if there was trouble, dealing only with Caesareans and emergency procedures. His midwives carried out most of the deliveries.

In France, to become a midwife or *sage-femme* – literally, 'wise woman' – you have to complete the first year of medical school, after which you're admitted to a special training course that takes a further four years. Like everything in the French education system, the course is extremely rigorous and theoretical. As well as learning the practical skill of delivering babies, the aspiring *sage-femme* has to study anatomy, physiology, pathology, microbiology, pharmacology, anaesthesiology, obstetrics, paediatrics, gynaecology, psychology and sociology, public health, law and, of course, sexology.

Hospitals have always been the core of the French healthcare system. This probably accounts for the extremely specialised, technical and curative nature of the healthcare. A medical report carried out in 2000 showed that after diagnosis of lung cancer, patients in Britain were twice as likely to die from the disease as they were in France. Sandrine, who is currently involved in a massive programme of reform of the French Health Service and who has travelled frequently to the UK to compare systems, explained that the reason for this therapeutic gap is not the quality of British practitioners but rather the lack of resources and the resulting waiting lists. Lung cancer has to be treated quickly otherwise there is little chance of survival. In France there are no waiting lists for this type of disease, so the patient is treated immediately after diagnosis. As a result, the survival rates for people with lung cancer five years after diagnosis are only 7 per cent in the UK and 14 per cent in France.

Because everything revolves around the hospital, there is virtually no community care in France. Once you leave hospital with your baby, you're pretty much on your own. There's no health visitor unless your neighbour denounces you to the social services, and as for home births, they are very rare and strongly discouraged. You would have to fight the very interventionist system that kicks in as soon as you become pregnant and which has you under close medical surveillance from start to finish. This includes monthly check-ups, endless blood tests, three obligatory scans and hospitalisation if there's even the hint of a premature birth. Once you've had your baby, you are kept in hospital for a minimum of three days, five to ten if you've had a Caesarean. As you get your own room, good food and the option of night-time care of your newborn from a staff of truly devoted men and women – all for free – this was not something I ever resisted. Each time I had a baby in France I came home completely restored.

Just before I left the hospital, I had a visit from a gynaecologist who asked me if I needed a prescription for some contraception. That dealt with, she handed me what appeared to be a vibrator. I asked her if this was a kind of going-home present from the French Public Health Service, and she smiled and said 'sort of'.

As it turned out, it was not a sex toy but a vaginal probe. I was to take it to my local *kiné*, short for *kinésithérapeute* or physiotherapist (of which there are huge numbers in France), and she, or he, would plug the other end into a machine that would send electrical impulses into the probe in order to tone and 're-educate' my perineum. When I had got over the shock of being handed such a rude-looking object, I was overcome with admiration at a society willing to pay for millions of women to tone their fannies in the aftermath of birth. In retrospect, it not only makes sense for the healthy sex life of the nation, it makes sense economically too. The health costs incurred by mass female incontinence must be higher than a few million vaginal probes and some sessions with the *kiné*.

When you get home from hospital, the compulsory visits to the paediatrician begin. He or she will strong-arm you into vaccinating your baby, endlessly weigh and measure him and plot his developmental progress on the various little graphs in the back of his precious medical 'log-book'. This *carnet de santé*, as it is called, is part of an elaborate system of professional surveillance that continues all the way through childhood. It was, I suppose, the first sign of a phenomenon that would become increasingly obvious to me: France loves norms, and this love is part of her identity.

I soon realised that this was extended to breastfeeding as well. When my first child was born I was asked by my midwife if I intended to breastfeed. She smiled encouragingly at me, adding 'bravo', and scribbled something on her clipboard. When I went on to say that I hoped to keep it up for at least nine months, her face fell.

'Nine months! That's not necessary. They get all they need in the way of immunity in three.'

This, clearly, was a universally acknowledged fact and explained why of the mothers who did choose to breast-feed, the vast majority stopped after three months. In France only about 55 per cent of mothers breastfeed, and because most of them return to work within the first six months, they tend to wean their babies early. I think, however, that the objection to late weaning runs much deeper. The reactions I got from my Parisian entourage when I allowed my ten-month-old boy to suckle at my breast at a dinner party were too violent for them to be purely practical.

'It's unnatural!' the inimitable Nathalie protested. 'He's got *teeth*!'

A few of the women present on that occasion were, I think, a little jealous that my work enabled me to go on breastfeeding when theirs had not. But, in most cases, they agreed with Nathalie that it was 'unnatural', expressing the deep-seated but unavowed conviction that breasts were first and foremost for sexual pleasure and the erotic delight of men.

Magali, who was seen by the other members of *la bande* as the most maternal among us – since she had been the first to have children, was the best cook and had a nurturing personality – had chosen not to breastfeed any of her three children. She once explained to me that her breasts were her best feature and that she didn't want to risk damaging them.

At the time her remark had struck me as selfish – immoral even. Surely that was what breasts were for? Of course there is always the risk of damage, with or without breastfeeding, but her husband should love them anyway and if he didn't, well . . . he was an arsehole. In retrospect, however, I can appreciate her point of view. Her breasts did indeed stay lovely for many years and her children didn't seem to suffer from having been bottle-fed. They appeared neither unhealthier nor more insecure than other children I knew who had been breastfed, since there are obviously plenty of ways to mess up your children after you've weaned them. Magali was clearly a devoted mother, and her choice was a happy, guilt-free one that has been beneficial to her sexual fulfilment and, by extension, to her whole family. The moral imperative that has come to surround breastfeeding in Britain may simply be another manifestation of puritan guilt and, as such, one that needs to be watched.

France is extravagant when it comes to healthcare spending, which represents just under 10 per cent of her gross domestic product. In 2000 the World Health Organisation ranked her healthcare system first among the 191 member countries surveyed, stating that it provided 'the best overall healthcare'. The health system in the US, which spends a higher portion of her GDP than any other country, ranked thirty-seventh. Britain, which spends 6 per cent of her GDP on the health service, ranked eighteenth.

The principle, ever since the French Public Health Insurance System was set up in 1945, has always been to provide unlimited access to care, patients being allowed to see as many physicians – including specialists for whom no referral is required – as often as they like. Compared to their British counterparts, French practitioners, even those working in the private sector, have always had a great deal of freedom over where they set up shop, how they function and what they prescribe, yet the bulk of their income is paid by public funds. As healthcare costs have continued to soar, this has become more and more of a concern. In recent years the French State has made a concerted effort to reduce costs – a delicate business since the lavish healthcare system is one of those 'privileges for all' that the French public is loath to relinquish.

On the surface, the system is both extravagant and chaotic. To qualify for health coverage you have to pay an insurance premium calculated as a percentage of your income. In addition to this, you pay fees for most things at the time of use, unless you earn below a certain income, in which case you are exempt. You then claim between 70 and 100 per cent of the fees back from your insurer. The result of this system is a very high standard of care available to everyone, without the waiting lists that characterise the NHS. Given that you can identify on your payslip how much you're paying for your healthcare, you can then form an opinion about whether or not the cost is justified. The system is a kind of compromise between egalitarianism and liberalism. All citizens are said to be equal, but choice and competition are fiercely protected. The insurer makes no distinction between public and private hospitals (which provide about 35 per cent of beds), and patients have complete freedom of choice.

There are, however, drawbacks to this extremely lavish system. And they are not just the obvious, economic ones relating to the ever-growing deficit (to which most French people, incidentally, are impervious). As my own experience would teach me, the effects of this munificent, normative and interventionist system have deeper and more far-reaching consequences. My firstborn, Jack, who was delivered without incident by one of Professor Minkowski's lovely midwives, would suffer from an early age as a result of this subtle but persistent normative pressure. From the moment we left the hospital, I would find myself constantly battling against professionals from all walks of French life who wished to intervene to help my son become . . . well . . . more like everyone else. It started with the paediatrician, who put a dissatisfied dot on the growth chart in the back of his *carnet de santé* and urged me to consider growth-hormone treatment, since it was plain to see, at the age of eighteen months, Jack was *hors norme* (outside the norm).

I refused the pituitary growth-hormone treatment that was available and being prescribed to children at the time, simply because I had been tiny for most of my childhood (my father had made me hang from door frames) and thought that Jack would probably have a late growth spurt as I had. As it turned out, the treatment being offered to us had a good chance of being contaminated with Creutzfeld-Jacob disease, and its administration to 1,500 children in France between February 1984 and February 1986 would become one of the biggest medical scandals of the decade; five people were arrested for not having taken the product out of circulation once it was known to be contaminated. The fifty deaths from this terrifying, debilitating disease which resulted from the French treatment programme represented more than half of all known cases worldwide and probably presaged many more.

The next battle on my son's behalf would be with a nursery-school teacher who announced that at his age he should no longer be drawing *hommes-têtards*, 'tadpole men'. By this she meant stick men without bodies but with arms and legs coming out of their heads. I listened in amazement as she told me that this was a sign of arrested development. She recommended he see the school psychiatrist. We were on the street when we had this conversation and I remember laughing out loud at her proposal.

'A psychiatrist!' I said. 'He's only three!'

'Madame,' she said gently. 'The sooner we deal with the problem, the better.'

When it became clear that I wasn't going to agree, her manner hardened.

'I think you should know that your son tends to place himself in the role of the victim,' she explained.

At the time I was aghast, but this kind of psychobabble would prove quite common among teachers, who used it to strike guilt and fear into the hearts of all parents whose children didn't fit the mould. Fighting this tendency towards the conformism inherent in French society took up a great deal of my energy as a mother.

One battle, which I actually lost, stands in retrospect as a kind of metaphor for all the minor battles I fought on behalf of my children's individuality. Once again, the fight was with a member of the medical profession and again it concerned my son and his so-called abnormality. At the age of fifteen, Jack had, like many of his contemporaries, a pronounced slouch, which has since disappeared. Seeing his posture one summer, Sandrine, the anaesthetist, kindly recommended a professor who had a stellar reputation and who would certainly be able to help.

The professor in question examined Jack and prescribed a corrective, fibreglass corset (I had hoped that a few t'ai chi lessons might do the trick) to be worn night and day for a minimum of two years. Jack was to wear this mortifying contraption until he was seventeen! I protested to Laurent that these were pivotal years for the development of his self-esteem. He would be starting to date girls. Wearing callipers on his chest wouldn't exactly help him pull.

But the professor had put the fear of God into Laurent. If Jack didn't wear the corset, he had warned, he would have to undergo drastic surgery, which would involve sawing through his spine at the neck. I gave in.

The corset was so constrictive that at first Jack couldn't sleep and would tear it off in the middle of the night – the crowning metaphor for a system that had always tried to confine him. In the end I stopped making him wear it. Laurent and I were separated by that time and the corset stayed in the cupboard, only to be brought out when Jack saw the professor or his father. After two years of this charade, the doctor announced that the results had been extremely satisfactory and that, thanks to the corset, we had eluded the worst. I could tell from Jack's expression that he was bursting to tell that smug little man that he had hardly ever worn it, but he stayed quiet.

8 Education

Freud, Maths and the Cult of Reason

When that nursery-school teacher had told me that my three-year-old had masochistic tendencies and invoked the psychiatrist, I was still sufficiently contaminated by my British scepticism to laugh. But as the years went by and I became more caught up in bourgeois Parisian society, the ubiquity of psychoanalytic theory began to work its spell on me. Many of my husband's friends were in analysis – mostly as an intellectual pastime – and would discuss their treatment at dinner parties, but always in the most abstract of terms. The conversation would never take on a personal note, as it would have on the Upper West Side of Manhattan. It would remain beautifully theoretical, like Bettelheim or Barthes or Derrida. For in this Catholic culture, what was interesting was not the personal or the symptomatic, but the collective and the universal.

Since May 1968, psychoanalysis – entirely dominated in France by Freudian theory – has exerted a considerable influence on all of society. Along with Marx, Freud was the emblematic figure of the '68 barricades. In the search for a viable alternative to Catholic values – one that would correspond to the deepest nature of the French people, with their obsession for order, hierarchy but, above all, gratification – Freudian theory, with its emphasis on the libido, was a perfect solution. The media – both low- and highbrow – have always spread the word, often wheeling out Freudians as experts on all aspects of society from the most banal to the most serious. Pioneered by *Elle* magazine, all women's magazines now have their resident Freudian analyst who will answer all your problems from sporadic orgasm to coping with your child to dealing with your lover. The psychiatrist affiliated to your child's school or university is invariably a Freudian, as is the hawk-eyed therapist attached to the local kindergarten who will keep watch over your toddler's drawings.

The theory of the unconscious, one of the most influential of the twentieth century, captured the French imagination in particular, due to the beauty of its all-encompassing nature. Freud's system never claimed to be scientific and as such cannot really be refuted. It is, as his disciples tend to show, a matter of faith. Like the Catholic Church before it, the *Société Psychanalytique de Paris* (SPP, the union of Freudian analysts in France) requires obedience as well as respect for tradition. It does not accept refutation or change. It is probably no coincidence that recent developments in psychotherapeutic techniques, which began by contesting Freudian hegemony, are thriving in Protestant societies and struggling in Catholic ones. As W. H. Auden put it in his essay on the Protestant mystics, if the Catholic approach to faith can be summed up by the words '*We* believe *still*',

Protestantism will always be a matter of '*I* believe *again*.'

Because of the dominance of Freudian theory, the revolution in therapeutic practices brought by more recent cognitive and behavioural therapies is decried in France, where they are seen as prosaic, limiting and quintessentially Anglo-Saxon. The pragmatic approach to mental illness, which tends towards the search for an alleviation of symptoms, does not seem to interest the French psychoanalytic community. In 2004 the SPP managed to put pressure on the French government to suppress a report by the state research institute, INSERM, which revealed the relative success of cognitive and behavioural therapies in curing mental illness.

As one Freudian analyst, Jacques-Alain Miller, a member of the SPP, explained: 'The patient arrives with symptoms and he finds throughout the course of the therapy that they are simply a screen onto which he is projecting his internal strife. Psychoanalysis doesn't mend his past but enables him to accept it. Because psychoanalysis is not a medical procedure, it is difficult to evaluate its success.'

To practitioners like Miller, the cure is not the point. For the small handful of pioneers attempting to spread cognitive, behavioural and other 'problem-solving' therapies in France, this kind of highly theoretical approach is a form of irresponsibility. For them, the role of the practitioner is not to enable the patient to accept his or her suffering but to work for a cure and provide some kind of accountability to the patient in the process. The idea of accountability, of course, infers an equal relationship between therapist and patient, who becomes, in some sense, a client receiving a service. For the analysts of the SPP, this contractual approach not only belittles the almost mystical experience of the psychoanalytic process but also diminishes the high-priestly status of the analyst.

Auden's observation of Protestant culture, which champions the *I* and the *Now* over the *We* and the *Then* of Catholic cultures, is nowhere more relevant than in France, where an enduring taste for collective worship is expressed in contemporary society through a passion for the Common Cause. French people are never happier than when their individuality is being dissolved in a movement, a street demonstration or a beautiful, all-embracing theory like that of Sigmund Freud.

As I would soon discover, the greatest rampart against individuality in French society is *L'Ecole Publique* (State school), and the most formidable guardians of the norm are the teachers therein. But I should not, as the French say, 'spit in the soup', by which I mean I should be grateful for what I have. When it comes to the education that my children have received at the hands of the French State, I would not, in retrospect, exchange it for the education that is available in Britain to my friends' children. My children were both, for all my elitist schooling, better educated than I was. They can do maths, for a start. They have a chronological and comprehensive sense of history, while I have a patchy one (confined mostly to Tudor Britain, Gladstone's army reforms and the Second World

War). They know the teachings of Western civilisation's key philosophers, from Plato to Descartes to Sartre. They have a decent understanding of how the immune system works and what a gene is, and they have a deep and extensive knowledge of French literature.

The reason for this is that from the age of six, they were burdened with unbelievable amounts of homework and saddled with all the things that modern British pedagogy decries: rote-learning, dictation, relentless competition and exams. They sometimes seemed to me like rats in a cage. There was hardly any sport or art and no drama. If they wanted to practise a sport, they could do so in their precious free time, on Wednesday afternoons, and if they did, it would tend to be in an atmosphere of fierce competition.

Before the French State took over the business of educating its children, schools in France were in the hands of the Church and, in particular, the Jesuits. St Ignatius de Loyola, the founder of the Jesuit order, believed in obedience as the key virtue and ordered total submission to the will of one's superiors. This hierarchical vision of education was championed by Napoleon, who had himself benefited from the rigours of Jesuit teaching methods and who set up a system of *lycées* that he dreamed would be run by 'Jesuits of the State'. It did not take me long to realise that Napoleon's dream had come true. For the teaching staff, my children were vessels to be filled. Their capacity to receive information was the sole measure of their success. No other criteria – not creativity, or imagination, or physical prowess – were used to assess their quality as human beings.

Nowhere is the French obsession for nobility more clearly reflected than in the education system, which is, despite its egalitarian philosophy, extremely hierarchical. The teaching body is divided between those who have passed the vertiginously difficult *agrégation* and are forever glorified in the eyes of society (no matter how lacking they may be in pedagogic skills) and those who have taken the more practical teacher-training programme, the CAPES (*Certificat d'Aptitude au Professorat de l'Enseignement du Second Degré*), and who are perceived as second-rate and treated as such in their careers. My son Jack, a survivor of and convert to the French education system, once tried to explain to me his urgent desire to sit the *agrégation*.

'If you pass it, Mum, and most people have to sit the exam at least three times before they do . . . But *if* you pass it, you never have to prove yourself again. You become an intellectual god.'

Beyond my surprise that a nineteen-year-old should aspire to such stasis was a sense of despair that my own child should have been so contaminated by France's obsession for intellectual status.

Behind Jack's explanation lies a shocking reality: that you can pass an exam in your early twenties, be shrouded in glory and never, ever be fired. In most societies a degree or diploma is a starting block after which the individual must prove his or her professional worth. In France the right academic qualification will set you up until retirement. French *lycées* are filled with these *agrégés*, literally 'whole' beings, dangerously imbued with their own sense of entitlement. These are the mandarins of French academia who, in the name of excellence, block any reform that might represent an attack on their status.

The student body is also divided: there are more or less noble paths – Academic versus Technological – and more or less noble disciplines – Maths and Sciences carry considerably more value than the Arts. Maths – in obedience to France's most influential philosopher, René Descartes – is the final arbiter of intelligence. But above all, Maths is seen as the great leveller. There is no need to come from a cultivated background to have an affinity for Maths. If you are blessed with a gift for numbers and at the age of sixteen choose the most prestigious of all the baccalaureate options, in which Maths carries the most weight, you are destined for greatness. Napoleon, who spoke poor, heavily accented French, excelled in Maths and was consequently able to succeed. Maths in France is the contemporary Latin. My daughter, who inherited her father's Maths brain, on entering the sixth form took it as the principal subject of her baccalaureate. She noted that her teacher strove to teach it in the most abstract way possible, keeping it as firmly divorced from the uses of everyday life as it could possibly be.

This attachment to an archaic and non-pragmatic pedagogy is compounded by a deep and lasting problem of denial. The republican obsession with equality means that no one – neither the politicians attempting educational reform, nor the teaching body itself – will ever admit to their underlying belief that some are more noble than others. This means that it is utterly impossible ever to tackle the reality of a diverse student population, or ever properly address the needs of those children in difficulty, especially if they happen to belong to an ethnic minority. Talk to a French secondary-school teacher, an *agrégé* employed by the Ministry of Education for life, and you will quickly hit the bedrock of their prejudice. Their huge self-importance, coupled with their egalitarian ideology, makes them despise notions like ethnicity, diversity or special needs. Perhaps part of the reason for this is that they lack the human gifts required for nurturing these children.

While my daughter Ella thrived on the extreme rigour of the system and always performed well in it, Jack was miserable from the start and did not. In Britain, I'm sure he would have been seen as a special-needs child and helped accordingly. Here in France he was placed in that ignominious category known as *en echec*, which means, quite simply, 'failing', and then – more shaming still – marked out for a *bilan psychologique* (psychological assessment). Laurent and I, unless we wanted Jack expelled, were forced to take him to Paris's main psychiatric hospital, Sainte-Anne, for close and gruelling psychiatric scrutiny.

As we walked with our eight-year-old through the lugubrious grounds, past the patients in their various postures of lunacy or distress, I inevitably wondered what we had done to our son to find ourselves in this situation. As it turned out, an analysis of Jack's drawings revealed that I had not allowed him sufficiently to regress. I was not sure what this meant, but at the time I felt terrible. It is, of course, a constant of Freudian analysis to look for the mother's role in the elaboration of complexes and repression. Long after autism was found to be an organic disorder, triggered by genetic factors, French mothers were still being blamed for their 'failure to bond' with their child. The myth of the 'refrigerator mother' who causes the autistic symptoms through her 'unconscious wish that the child should not exist' was propagated by theorists like Dr Bruno Bettelheim and echoed by the French psychoanalytic community for decades. Even today there are plenty of French analysts who refuse to accept the biological nature of autism and continue to compound the anguish of families with autistic children by apportioning blame. I know of one such family who ten years ago moved to London because behavioural therapy for autism simply did not exist in France. In this case the mother was sufficiently strong to resist the temptation to believe that her son's condition was all her fault.

Jack was a dreamer and for this he would be punished for years. He also loved abstraction and this would ultimately equip him very well for tertiary education in France, provided he could stay the course. In his last year of secondary school, Jack, along with the rest of his class, discovered philosophy and he became very good at it. But in all the previous years, the system judged and condemned him. At the age of seven, that symbolic age for Freudians when the 'repressive phase' begins, the age which the Jesuits used to call 'the age of reason', Jack was expected to be alert, receptive and able to absorb, without questioning, huge quantities of facts. On the one hand, the French school system insisted that he emerge from the dream of childhood, and on the other, the psychiatric establishment was telling me to let him go back there. At the time, I was lost, consumed with guilt and endlessly worried about my son.

Branded with the stigma of the 'failing child', under frequent psychiatric supervision, Jack struggled on like this for years until in the end he got fed up and left school in his final year, taking his baccalaureate by correspondence at the age of eighteen and passing. His talent for philosophy got him into the Sorbonne and he has never looked back.

Bizarrely, Jack now swears by the French school system and won't hear a word against it, not because it didn't make him miserable at the time, but because he believes it instilled in him a rigour and a desire for excellence that he would not have had otherwise. I'm not in a position to judge if he's right or wrong, but I don't think I'm prepared to go through the same experience with my younger children if, when it's time for them to go to school, they too prove to be dreamers.

Jack survived, but I don't know how many of his kind do. Neither the French education system nor the society beyond it champions the imagination. I believe that it is no coincidence that neither of my elder children have chosen to work in the Arts, which they, along with most of their peers, perceive as sacred and reserved for the lucky few, but not a viable means of making a living. Indeed, it is a wonder to me that novels even get written or art ever made in a culture that worships reason and knowledge to this degree. Experience, the raw material of the imagination, is not valued in this society. Ideas are, and, as a result, contemporary French literature is dominated by members of an academic elite. The novels that are published tend to be stylistically elegant, driven by a deep love of the language and, as far as narrative is concerned, pretty impoverished: story, like personal experience, is a dirty word.

This is, I think, yet another of Catholicism's cultural legacies: Auden's Catholic *We* versus the Protestant *I*. It is also one that is under threat from Anglo-Saxon influences. In recent years there has been a backlash against the perceived elitism of French contemporary literature. Unsurprisingly, the iconoclasts have been mostly women and, unsurprisingly again, their subject matter has been mostly sex. Since the late nineties the confessional novel has made a comeback in the form of explicit memoirs by women about their sex lives. Novels like *Inceste* by Christine Angot, *Jouir* (Climax) by Catherine Cusset, *Viande* (Meat) by Claire Legendre or *The Sex Life of Catherine M* by Catherine Millet have been dismissed in more traditional literary circles as 'porno-chic', but they achieved huge success with readers eager for real-life accounts and proper stories. They also offer a vibrant alternative to the polished, hermetic works that have dominated the literary prizes in this country for so long.

Protestantism, in its relation to faith, emphasises personal experience. There is no intermediary between the Protestant and his God, and the absence of ritual in the context of worship suggests that the relationship with the deity should be internal and private rather than collective and social. The often beautiful Catholic rites that persist in countries like Italy and Spain – the cults of the Madonna and the local saint – were destroyed by the French Revolution, but there is an enduring nostalgia for institutional cults and collective worship which I am sure explain the utterly unfathomable French taste for *son et lumière*.

This love of ritual may explain why reality TV has not taken hold in France. French versions of programmes like *Big Brother* tend to be obviously staged and revolve around archaic, fairy-tale scenarios like looking for a rich husband (*Eric le Millionnaire*) or trying to become a pop star (*Star Academy*). Britain has, of course, drifted in the opposite direction but somehow managed to end up in the same place: in our thirst for the personal account, we've made a cult out of reality; but as our culture becomes more and more voyeuristic, the viewed experience becomes increasingly doctored or processed, and what we call reality becomes the kind of false, self-dramatising posturing of a nation of adolescents endlessly acting out their narcissistic tendencies.

My first job in France was as an assistant to a professor of English at Saint-Denis University in the outskirts of Paris. Saint-Denis is a suburb. In French the word is *banlieue*, which means literally 'place of banishment', an apt description for many of these areas that are forsaken by the police, social and public services, or anyone who represents authority. The tower blocks of places like Saint-Denis, euphemistically dubbed *les cités*, in echo of antiquity, are inhabited mostly by immigrants, 'invited' from francophone Africa and the Maghreb during the sixties and seventies by Presidents Pompidou and Giscard d'Estaing to build France's magnificent infrastructure. It is the French-born children and grandchildren of these workers who, with their formidable rioting, periodically put the fear of God into France's politicians and, indeed, those members of the Parisian bourgeoisie who have the imagination to realise that there is nothing separating them from the ire of these disaffected youths but Paris's ring road.

Saint-Denis University, or 'Paris 8' as it is known, was created at the end of 1968. It used to be known by the rather Maoist name of *L'Université Populaire* and was initially an 'experimental faculty', focusing mainly on soft sciences like philosophy and sociology, with a voluntarily anti-academic perspective. The illustrious names that made up the first teaching body include Gilles Deleuze and Michel Foucault (who set up the Philosophy department) and Hélène Cixous (who introduced Women's Studies, still taught nowhere else in France). These people lent the place the extremely theoretical and politicised aura that persists today.

Like most of France's public universities, Paris 8 has no selection criteria. Anyone with the baccalaureate can enter, but few stay the course. The drop-out rate for philosophy at the Sorbonne in the first year, for instance, is huge; only about 30 per cent of those admitted go through to the second year. Students are left entirely to their own devices and receive no guidance from their professors, who tend to behave like rock stars, entirely inaccessible for advice. Magisterial lectures are held in vast, over-crowded auditoriums. As with the school system, only the self-motivators who are naturally rigorous and conscientious survive (or else the handful of monomaniacs like my son, motivated by their thirst for revenge on a system that has tried to crush them). The French university system is a matter of sink or swim. If you can stay afloat for three years – and those who do so invariably go on to do a Masters, since a simple bachelor's degree carries little value on the French job market – then you will receive a first-rate, though entirely impractical, education that has hardly changed since the eighteenth century.

My first day as an assistant teacher at Saint-Denis was with a group of third-year students of English, many of them clinging on by the skin of their teeth. They were all there because they wanted to be there and they worked hard. My job was to interview them about themselves one by one and note down the different categories of expression – narrative, experiential, descriptive, objective, discursive, theoretical – in an attempt to identify and reveal to them where their linguistic strategies lay. It was a pseudo-scientific approach to the learning of a language that now strikes me as typically French.

In the process, however, I discovered something interesting – all of them were afraid of talking about their own experiences. They had been very effectively formatted to avoid two of the categories I was testing them for: the experiential and the descriptive. None of them were comfortable with demands like 'describe where you live'. All of them slipped into generalities about the socio-economic profile of the inhabitants of their particular *quartier* or confined themselves to opinions about how pleasant or unpleasant the place was.

Most of their sentences, I noticed, began with 'I think', as though they felt that what was required of them was a well-honed opinion. It was impossible to get them to *describe* anything. Description calls upon the imagination and the will to mould reality for the entertainment of the listener. As I would later discover with my own children, pupils in France are hardly ever asked to do this. Descartes's fantasy – to extend mathematical enquiry to all fields of human knowledge – was clearly working here, even among the children of France's immigrants.

Smiley, Happy People

Running parallel with the hegemony of Freudian psycho-analysis in France is the widespread use of the anti-depressant. The French are the biggest consumers of psychotropic drugs in the world. Contrary to popular belief, they far outstrip the Americans. Recent research by scientists from Bordeaux found that almost a quarter of all French, more than 15 million people, admitted to having taken either anti-depressants or tranquillisers in the past year – five times as many as in Britain and a third more than in America.

In Laurent's bourgeois Parisian entourage, I would say that the proportion of people regularly using these drugs was considerably higher than that. There is no taboo surrounding the use of tranquillisers like *Lexomil* and *Tranxène*, which are offered over café tables by ladies who lunch when one of them is experiencing a *coup de blues* at her husband's most recent affair. GPs tend to prescribe these drugs at the drop of a hat. Recently, two female journalists from the medical newspaper *Le Quotidien du Médecin* consulted sixty GPs across France, claiming to have stress and anxiety symptoms, and reported that every single practitioner prescribed them with tranquillisers.

On the other hand, French people with severe psychiatric problems, including psychosis, do not always get drugs, especially if they are in therapy. Therapists in France are generally trained doctors who have then specialised in psychiatry. Theoretically, they can all prescribe drugs, but since most of them are Freudians they tend to decry the use of medication, which they believe interferes with the therapeutic process. So Laurent's friends who were under psychoanalysis didn't tell their shrinks what they were getting from their GPs. If you're an averagely neurotic patient with time and money on your hands, a French GP will feel relaxed about supplying you with prescriptions for tranquillisers or anti-depressants for as long as you like. If you're poor, however, or psychotic, or both, French GPs tend to play safe and refer you to a psychiatric hospital.

The widespread use of these drugs does not alter the fact that France has one of the highest suicide rates in Europe. According to OECD figures, approximately seventeen out of every hundred thousand French people take their own lives each year, compared to seven Britons. You might ask why – in a society where the quality of life seems to be superior, where fertility and life expectancy and literacy are higher, where the crime rate is lower and teenage pregnancies fewer – so many people want to kill themselves . . .

Having raised my children in this society, I have a number of theories of my own – none of them particularly conclusive – but they all relate to the various myths and fantasies that seem to inhabit the French and condition their approach to suffering. All the values that form the bedrock of France's collective unconscious – the Cult of Beauty, the Tragic (rather than the Comic) world view, the Cult of Reason – leave French people particularly ill-equipped for the harsher aspects of reality. Suffering, when it occurs, must be sublime. It cannot be of the petty, miserable, shabby variety. It has to be grandiose and romantic. The historic example of Napoleon's slow and ignominious death on the island of Saint Helena is cited by the French as indicative of the ingenious cruelty of the British. Wedded to the nuts and bolts of reality as we are, we refused him the noble, transcendent death for which he was destined by slowly poisoning him.

Suicide is a serious matter and throwing out idle theories based on little more than intuition is a dangerous business, but I can't help feeling that a culture which champions the sublime, the grand and the noble, sets up impossible standards for its citizens. What is existentialism – a philosophy born out of the particular tension between the *idea* of being French and the reality – but the desire to opt out of these impossible standards and reinvent your existence with each passing moment? Surely suicide, in a culture such as this, is a form of sublimation, a means of regaining control over the quagmire that is reality. Gilles Deleuze, one of the great thinkers of twentieth-century France, threw himself out of a window. Richard Pinhas, one of Deleuze's most eager disciples, who made an academic website devoted to his thought, described Deleuze's suicide as 'his final act of liberty'.

All cultures have their own particular ways of fabricating meaning. British culture is a strange alchemy produced by the continual confrontation between custom and rebellion, between the old and the new. It is a cultural model that functions relatively well in the modern world. French culture, with its rigid founding myths, its obsession for nobility and status, is particularly ill-suited to the hurtling flux of globalisation.

The French tend not to use the word depression lightly. People don't say, 'I'm really depressed this week,' because in France, having a hard time is not a badge of honour unless it happens to be suffering on a grand scale. Ask a French person how they are and they will never answer: bored, depressed, hung-over, broke, fat or spotty. They'll put a brave face on their misery and say, '*Ça va . . . Plutôt bien . . .*' And then they'll change the subject, ideally to something abstract, like politics or cinema or art.

As I soon discovered, a considerable number of Laurent's friends were on anti-depressants. Some of them were clinically depressed and others were simply not interested in the particular lows that go with being alive. The normative principle in France – which begins at *maternelle* and carries on relentlessly all through childhood – means that the pressure to keep up appearances is considerable. This pressure makes intimacy a rare commodity and explains why, after twenty years in a country that I have come to love, there are still no French people with whom I share the openness of my English friendships.

When I first moved to Paris, I was struck by the gap I kept encountering between what was preached and what was practised. People were always banging on about *solidarité* and yet they didn't know or care to know the other people in their building. For all her talk of fraternity and its modern equivalent, solidarity, France is a monumentally individualistic society. Her political system facilitates a certain detachment from her outcasts and high levels of taxation redeem the consciences of her citizens. And so the millions of unemployed and dispossessed on the fringes of all her big cities can be forgotten . . . At least until the next time they rise up in protest.

When Laurent and I rented our first flat together, I went and knocked on doors to introduce myself to my neighbours on the other floors. I was greeted first by mistrust – I must be a Jehovah's Witness – then, when they discovered that I was English, amusement and good will. Yes, I was English and therefore to be forgiven, admired even, for my eccentricity.

For the sad truth is that, for all our French-bashing, we are in fact loved by the French. They love our eccentricity, they love our sense of humour; they love our moral courage, our excess, our restraint and our imagination.

Laurent's despondency on returning home after watching the English rugby team beat the French team in their Stade de France offers a good idea of most Frenchmen's view of their own countrymen as compared to the English.

'As usual the English chants gave me goose pimples and our doleful "*Allez les Bleus*" sounded like a band of snotty, undisciplined brats, just like our players were in the face of the impeccable order of the English game.'

If they could, many French people would gladly

exchange their character for ours, be rid of their earnest intellectualism, their conformism, their indiscipline, their petulance, their pusillanimity and their bigotry. But there is a problem: these are the very traits which lie behind the extraordinary quality of their lives, the quality which people like Peter Mayle help us to drool over and for which thousands of Britons abandon their long-suffering island every year.

9 The Past

The Discreet Charm of the Bourgeoisie

Laurent and I settled with our new baby into his small flat in Montmartre overlooking the gardens of the Sacré Cœur. Armed with my vaginal probe, I went for my bi-weekly sessions with the *kinésithérapeute* and succumbed to pressure from *la bande* to stop breastfeeding Jack after three months. I also became inured to the practice of medicating my child through the bottom. I now consider the widespread use of suppositories in France as sensible, rather than rude. The body absorbs medicine more quickly this way and bypassing the stomach makes perfect sense, particularly for children who can vomit easily or refuse to take medicine orally. Today, what I find suspect is the Anglo-Saxon hysteria surrounding the idea of suppositories.

Often Laurent and I would get a babysitter from a company called *Alpha Bébé* and go out to dinner with his friends, usually in noisy, brightly lit brasseries, and I would cling on to the edges of comprehension as they discussed the function of Art or the death of History or whatever happened to be the zeitgeist of the week.

Jack cried a lot at night, and as my own mother was in

Australia and usually asleep when I needed her, I sought
the advice of Laurent's friend Magali – the one who had
chosen not to breastfeed her children. She suggested
Théralène to ease Jack's nights, and our own. Years later
I'm appalled by the fact that I was actually giving a liquid
tranquilliser to a four-month-old baby and often wonder
if the addictive tendencies that plagued Jack's adolescence
were not due to this early exposure to narcoleptic sub-
stances.

It was April 1986 and I was beginning to miss my
friends back at Oxford. While I was out in the Paris spring,
shopping with my baby and learning how to choose in-
season vegetables with enough authority that the greengro-
cer didn't try to choose them for me, I thought of my
friends, eating jacket potatoes with baked-bean-and-
cheddar topping from the 'Spud-U-Like' van. While I was
learning how to avoid being given the worst cuts of meat
by the butcher, or how to greet *la boulangère*, not with
friendliness but with the routine civility that she expected
of me (ideally, one's *'Bonjour Madame!'* should be sung
with the cloying enthusiasm of a nursery-school teacher), I
imagined that my friends would be reading *Paradise Lost* in
front of their bar heaters or perusing manuscripts with
fingerless mittens in the Bodleian, or getting fall-down
drunk, or shagging each other in damp rooms with their
underwear drying comfortingly on the radiator, or dancing
to Chaka Khan . . . I missed my student life; having longed
to escape from it, of course, I missed it.

One weekend, David, a friend from Oxford, came to

stay. Laurent and I took him to a dinner party given by Aurélie and her boyfriend. The dinner party was held in the same flat, belonging to Aurélie's boyfriend, Daniel, which Laurent had staked out in the aftermath of their break-up. Daniel was the same boyfriend who had been kept awake all night by the sound of Laurent pleading outside on his doormat. One of the difficulties for me about all this lay in the fact that it was impossible to imagine my stable, rational husband ever behaving like this about me. His claim to have grown up since Aurélie was no consolation.

Like all of the women in *la bande*, Aurélie was a good and effortless cook. A long table ran the length of Daniel's garret flat and the little dormer windows were soon steamed up with conviviality. Daniel's lugubrious grey-and-mauve paintings – mostly, as far as I could tell, of couples involved in serious car crashes – hung on every available wall, and Aurélie, wearing a dress that looked like her perfect body had simply been wrapped in black bandages, flirted with the men and the women with equal commitment, lavishly kissing both on the lips. She was excited about a set of chairs she had made, entirely out of cardboard, as part of her course at Camondo, one of Paris's leading interior-design schools. In retrospect, those chairs showed real, even prophetic talent. Sadly Aurélie – who always had her eye on what she considered to be the main game (the Game of Love) – was always too busy with the pressures of adultery to fully live up to her professional potential.

The wine flowed, it didn't gush. People sipped, they didn't quaff. The evening seemed to be all about men and women and the games they play to entertain each other. In this context, inebriation felt inappropriate, even point-less, since if you became too drunk you would miss the fun. As my poor, dazed English friend would soon dis-cover, *all the fun* would turn out to be the discreet to-ing and fro-ing between the dinner table and the divan in the next-door room. What began as a *ménage à trois* (two girls and a boy) became *quatre* (two boys and two girls), then *cinq* (three boys and two girls) and, at the point when we went home to 'liberate the babysitter' – a *ménage à six*.

I noticed that people kept disappearing into the little room and assumed that somebody was showing a film they had made or perhaps watching a Formula 1 race. David seemed happy talking to someone else, so I stood up and went to have a look. I cannot remember the exact anatomical details but I did register my friend Betty (the one who saw a hypnotist for her climaxing difficulties) in a semi-naked, human knot with a small, male architect (the one who had learnt his English from Monty Python records) and a female psychiatric nurse (who had already frightened David during dinner by asking him if he liked having sex with strangers). Betty looked up and smiled sweetly at me and asked if I would like to join them. I said, 'No, no, I'm fine,' as coolly as I could and closed the door behind me.

My heart racing from the embarrassment, I sat down again next to David, wondering whether I should tell him what I had just seen. I remember looking across the table at Laurent and trying to decipher whether or not he was aware of what was going on in that little room. Later on, a man emerged from the room and came over to whisper something in Laurent's ear. Laurent shook his head, rather as if he were declining a cigar. Then he looked across at me and gave me a cosy smile.

Poor Laurent drove home that night to the sound of David and I squealing like a couple of schoolchildren. What astounded us most was the fact that there had been no drugs at the party and no one had seemed particularly drunk. How had this understated debauchery come about without the usual disinhibitors? In retrospect, what strikes me as uniquely French about that evening was not the fact of several people having sex together, but the rather elegant spontaneity of it all. There had been no need for such strategies of disassociation as the Key Game or Strip Poker, or indeed any kind of erotic formalisation. It had just been a matter of allowing the charge – that can come about when men and women are confined to a steamy room with good food and good wine – simply to take effect.

French Rudeness, Surrender and Betrayal

The early days of my married life were spent learning how to negotiate my way through the thick, plastic abattoir curtain of Parisian rudeness, without responding to every incident with an unsightly and ineffectual emotional display. I learnt that you did not show weakness or you would be shat upon, and that being overtly friendly or polite is widely perceived, in Paris at least, as a form of weakness. I learnt that there is a kind of behaviour that must be offered in lieu of politeness or friendliness. This behaviour is, I believe, a technique developed to mask social inequality, to gloss over any differences in status that would be uncomfortable to both parties.

The behaviour, adopted when one person is supposed to be 'serving' another, is a kind of formulaic banter in which each person says his or her lines and then moves on, entirely unscathed by the milk of human kindness. A decent knowledge of the language is essential for this banter (which of course puts foreigners at a considerable disadvantage). The ritual serves for many occasions, from buying a baguette to ordering coffee to dealing with the administration. If you don't have the words, then you don't have a chance. It's as simple as that. *The right words* show that you have reached a certain level in the social hierarchy and, at the same time, disguise the possibility that you might have risen above that level. They make possible the uncomfortable business of servitude in a society wedded to the myth of equality. It took me about ten years to learn this meta-language, which has its essential written version and without which it is hard to get anywhere in France.

This language is at once simple and complex. It insists upon the right delivery – in men, a detached indifference, and in women, a kind of singsong, pseudo-bonhomie, which amounts to the same thing. In this

aping of politeness, you don't so much talk *to* your inter-
locutor as *at* them.

This defensive approach to communication is, I suspect, the result of the particular cruelty for which French
society has periodically shown itself capable. History has
taught the French not to trust each other. Indeed, at various times in her past, France's citizens could not be
trusted *not* to denounce each other to the authorities –
were they royal, revolutionary or Nazi. This habit of mistrust forms the bedrock of her society. It explains why
Parisians never talk to each other in bus queues (except, of
course, during a general strike) and why they never share a
taxi.

In those early years in Paris, as I struggled to learn
what was of course innate to most French people, Laurent
was my champion and my defender. How many hours a
week did he spend writing, in that meta-language that he
uses so eloquently, to heads of Parisian department stores?
Or reporting taxi drivers to their employers for having
driven off while a pregnant English woman, with a child
in a pram and three bags of shopping, watched the
quicker, less burdened client climb in the other side? How
many times did he write on my behalf to lament the mis-
treatment of me and countless other poor foreigners suck-
ing their bloody fingernails as they clawed at the tower of
the French administration? Five times I had to return to
that citadel of bureaucratic impenetrability, the Préfecture
de Police, in my quest for a resident permit (*carte de
séjour*), which, incidentally, European citizens no longer

need. I would return each time with the missing piece of paperwork and peer, hopeful and teary-eyed, through the scratched plexiglass at the stinging indifference of the civil servant in charge of my *dossier*. I'd watch in trepidation as he or she pulled out that pink list of required documents and with a deep sigh, which could have been either pleasure or exasperation, scratched a deep cross with his or her biro beside one more missing element, to be brought back on the prescribed date in a month's time. A month later I would be back to wait my turn on the hard benches – on one occasion for four hours.

Years later I returned to this place, aglow with good intentions, in order to apply for French nationality. General elections were coming round again and it was time for me to take a stand, particularly in view of the fact that my own children had recently reached voting age. I walked into the old room – with its strip lighting and its peeling paintwork and its particular smell of bleach and damp wood – this time armed with the right language and attitude and ready to dish back whatever indignity I was served. A woman in her fifties with glasses on a string greeted me, or more accurately, came as close to shunning me as possible without actually turning her back on me. While I explained that I had lived in the country for twenty years, had had four children here and would like to apply for citizenship, she managed to make me feel that I was wasting her time. I cut my preamble short and asked her what the formalities were.

'On what grounds are you applying?'

'On what grounds?'

'On what grounds,' she repeated wearily.

'I would like to become French,' I said firmly. 'As I have said, I've been here . . .'

'Those aren't grounds. Anyone could come to this country illegally, stay for twenty years and ask to become French.'

She glanced at the clock on the wall. It was ten to twelve: nearly lunchtime.

I could feel the old anger and humiliation. I could feel myself being pulled back into the dark vortex of that core experience . . .

'What grounds do I need?'

'Are you married to a French national?'

'I was.'

'I asked if you were married. If you're no longer married, then the answer is no.'

I was now awash with anger, my head clamouring with the wrong words.

She pulled a form from beneath the counter and slid it towards me.

'Fill that in and bring back two copies. Your request will be assessed and if your dossier is complete and your request valid you'll be called for an interview.'

'Could you tell me how long this process usually takes?'

She answered me without looking up.

'If everything is in order, about two years.'

Then she pulled out the dreaded list of paperwork and put deep crosses beside every document.

I looked down at the list and felt a wave of calm. Then I looked up at her and said: 'You know what? I would like to thank you. I'm grateful to you for having cleared something up for me. Your behaviour, your particular kind of rudeness, has made me realise that I have no wish to become French after all.'

'Good,' she said, taking back the forms with a flourish. And without further ado, she turned off her desk lamp, took her jacket from her chair, opened the door of her booth and vanished from my life.

I have heard many theories about the reasons for Parisian rudeness but, for me, the most plausible lies in the city's history. The Franco-American writer Julian Green, who was born in Paris in 1900 and died there in 1998, once said of his city that she had lost her soul during the Nazi Occupation. Indeed, the now legendary incivility of Parisians seems to be a relatively recent phenomenon. Between the wars Paris was 'gay Paree', a dazzling place of creativity, hope and intellectual and sexual freedom. It was the extravagantly permissive city of Jean Rhys and Tristan Tzara and André Breton; the literary mecca of André Gide and Marcel Proust; the intellectual capital of the world, where Joyce could publish *Ulysses* and Gertrude Stein and Francis Scott Fitzgerald and Marianne Moore and Ernest Hemingway could make their dollars last long enough to reinvent American literature. It was the haven of artistic genius that nurtured Picasso, Matisse, Braque and Fernand Léger. It was a cultural melting pot where jazz could flourish . . . All this until the Occupation.

Paris is beautiful, elegant and bountiful. That is her essence. She is not meant for hardship, ugliness and toil. Whenever she is tested by reality, she fails. For Julian Green, it was the hardship of occupation that turned her into the cold, haughty, imperious museum that she is today. Perhaps the daily indignities and betrayals of life under the Nazis took the Parisians to a level of cruelty from which they have never returned. What is certain is that the French bourgeoisie, *grande* and *petite*, did not behave well under the Occupation. Denis Rake, an English spy who was dropped into Occupied France and whose work with the Resistance brought him into contact with many different sections of the population, always spoke very highly of the French working classes. When questioned by Marcel Ophüls in his documentary *Le Chagrin et la Pitié* (*The Sorrow and the Pity*) about the bourgeois Parisians he met under the Occupation, Rake remains evasive, saying that he learnt quickly not to expect their help. 'They had more to lose, I think,' he said generously.

Paris under the Nazis seems to have become a place of betrayal and denunciation. Proof of widespread ignominy can be found in the city's archives, which are filled with thousands of anonymous letters, addressed to both the French and German authorities, in which the writer denounces his or her neighbour, colleague or acquaintance, sometimes as a communist but most frequently as 'a member of the Jewish race'. Generally written to the Prefect, the letters tended to begin with the following: 'It is my honour to bring to your attention the facts which follow . . .'

Reading the unctuous tone of these letters, it is chilling to think that in a matter of days, the SS, the *Police Nationale* or the French *Milice* would have shown up at the address provided, arrested the individual and, wherever possible, his or her entire family, confiscated their belongings and requisitioned their apartment, taken them to the French internment camp of Drancy, put them on a French train and sent them to be exterminated in Poland or Germany.

These letters of denunciation, 55 million of them, were found in the French and German archives, many of them three or four decades after the war. Until the seventies, there was an embargo on information surrounding the degree of France's complicity in the deportation of her Jews. De Gaulle had instigated a policy of 'wiping the slate clean' (*passer l'éponge*), essential, as he saw it, for national reconciliation. In the years following the Occupation, there was one of those recurring upsurges of violence to which French history is prone, and which we are not allowed to call civil war, even though a war between political factions within the same country is precisely what began in June 1944, while the Allies were busy liberating France. *L'épuration* (purge) ended in 1947, just as the Cold War was beginning.

France's post-war 'purge' was particularly savage. All

the myriad rivalries and jealousies that can inhabit any nation's towns and villages rose to the surface as Gaullists, communists and Pétainists battled for supremacy in a barbaric display of national retribution. Collaborators were denounced, then tortured or hanged or shot by dubious public tribunals. Women who were supposed to have slept with German officers were dragged half naked into village squares and ritually humiliated by having their heads shaven. But in many regions, the purges reached far beyond collaborators to include political undesirables and 'class enemies'. Of the ten thousand or so executions that were carried out during the *épuration*, only 791 were legally pronounced death sentences. When it became clear that in many cases these judgements were in fact the French Communist Party (PCF) clearing the path to revolution, de Gaulle began a smear campaign that blamed the communists for all the excesses of the purge, and the Popular Tribunals abruptly ceased.

After de Gaulle's death in 1970 it came as a shock, to France's youth in particular, to discover the extent of the nation's commitment to Pétain's collaborationist regime. Contrary to the Gaullist myth of a massively resisting nation, the French were predominantly supportive of the 'victor of Verdun' – at least until November 1942, when the Germans invaded the South, the hitherto unoccupied 'Free Zone'. The image with which Laurent and his generation had grown up was of legions of brave French men and women in berets, cycling across the French countryside at night to feed Jews hiding in barns or English aviators hiding in attics. After de Gaulle died, a series of films – the most famous of which was Max Ophüls's long-censored *Le Chagrin et la Pitié* – offered a different picture of France under the Occupation and led to decades of guilt and self-recrimination.

Since those years of mass *mea culpa* there has been a readjustment, and, as my own children's history books show, a more level view of France's war record has been established. It has become clear that those 55 million letters of denunciation were written by about 3 million people (many informers must have scribbled furiously right the way through the war). A large number of these people seem to have been making the most of the Vichy regime's repressive climate in order to eliminate a professional or romantic rival. This does not make these acts any less repulsive but it does put France's participation in the Shoah into a more realistic context.*

It was thanks to Laurent's mother, Madeleine, that I began to get a sense of the enduring legacy of the war on this culture. She spoke of the Nazi Occupation of Paris as if it were yesterday and, unlike my own mother's memories of the Blitz, there was not a trace of nostalgia. There was nothing romantic about Madeleine's memories. No process of sublimation or rewriting of the past had taken place in the intervening years. The harsh facts were undeniable.

* In Poland the Holocaust took more than 3 million Jewish lives and 8 per cent survived, while in France seventy-five thousand Jews died and 72 per cent survived.

France, in spite of her grandiose system of defence, her impenetrable Maginot Line and her superior firepower, had been entirely overrun by the enemy in five weeks. Hitler consummated France's defeat by making her sign the armistice in the very railway car in which the Germans had signed their surrender in 1918. As my children's text-book would put it, she had suffered 'the greatest military defeat in her history'.

Madeleine, whose mother had died in childbirth, was brought up by her grandmother. Madame de Segonzac was convinced, along with much of the nation, by Philippe Pétain's credentials as the man to preserve France's honour. In this, as in many other details, Madeleine's wartime experiences were quite representative of the rest of the Parisian bourgeoisie. They spent their war in Paris's sixteenth arrondissement, the Nazis' preferred quarter, living on the same avenue as the Gestapo head-quarters. Madeleine remembers feeling hungry much of the time, remembers, as well, her fear and hatred of the German uniform. She recalls listening, terrified, to the Allied bombing of nearby Boulogne and, at the age of eight, watching three of her Jewish classmates being called aside in assembly and marched away, never to be seen again.

In the four years prior to the Liberation, Madeleine's aunt and uncle were deported to Ravensbruk and Dachau for having hidden an English pilot (who had talked under torture). Like many French people, Madeleine's grand-mother had been shocked and appalled by Churchill's decision to destroy the French fleet in the port of Mers-el-Kebir in June 1940 rather than run the risk of letting it fall into enemy hands. It was a savage attack. The French fleet, trapped in the harbour, was unable to riposte and 1,297 French sailors died at the hands of their allies, having fired hardly a shot. All France's latent Anglophobia rose to the surface; the act was seen as yet another manifestation of English treachery. The fact that the Frenchman in command of the fleet at Mers-el-Kebir, Admiral Gensoul, had been given warning of the attack and numerous options for averting it made no difference. In its aftermath anti-English posters appeared all over Paris depicting an evil-looking Churchill grinning over the crosses of the French dead.

Admiral Somerville, the commander of the British fleet at Mers-el-Kebir, had been against the attack from the first. He had feared that destroying the fleet would throw the French into the arms of the Germans and had suggested at least allowing the French to put to sea and attacking them offshore, a move that would have had the merit of allowing the extremely proud Admiral Gensoul to save face. Years later, Somerville still referred to the attack as 'the biggest political blunder of modern times' and 'an absolutely bloody business'. Occurring only a few weeks after Churchill's idealistic proposal, in the aftermath of France's defeat, for an 'indissoluble union' between the two countries, the event made Franco-British relations as bad as they had ever been.

Like most French people, Madeleine's grandmother,

Madame de Segonzac, had never heard of Charles de Gaulle and missed his famous 'call to arms' when it was broadcast from London on 18 June 1940. The Mers-el-Kebir massacre, which took place just over two weeks later, made de Gaulle's task of recruiting Frenchmen to fight alongside Englishmen much more difficult. For Madame de Segonzac, such an idea seemed absurd and dangerous, and de Gaulle vain and insubordinate. Like most people of her generation, she had no wish to see German uniforms return to France. She did, however, believe that signing the armistice was the only realistic solution. For as long as she could, she blamed Vichy's excesses on Pétain's swarthy, inelegant prime minister, Pierre Laval. Indeed, Pétain had such credit with his countrymen that there are still people today entirely unwilling to accept the fact that it was not Laval but Pétain, with his fantasy of building an authoritarian revolution on the back of defeat, who was the true architect of Vichy's fascist policies.

I only have to compare my own mother's childhood with that of my mother-in-law to understand the profound differences between the English and French sense of history. Madeleine and all of her generation perceive history as flawed, ambiguous and barbarous in its contingency. The children brought up in England during the war – both country children and evacuees – were able to conserve a sense of history as being morally coherent. They watched the virtues of honour and fortitude win through in the end. France's war children, on the other hand, witnessed nothing but defeat, fear and moral cowardice. The forces of occupation were very effective in smothering the rare examples of heroism and, when they could not, they handpicked innocent men from the community and shot them in the village square.

I am often struck by the harshness with which my parents' generation, whose war was comparatively gentle, judge the French. Indeed, the fountainhead of anti-French sentiment that I so frequently detect in my own father seems to lie right there, in France's war experience – the main grievance being her swift defeat. They let us down badly, my father says. Why did they buckle so easily? Surely they chose to capitulate, in order to save the furniture? Why wasn't Paris destroyed like London was? Because the French care more about Beauty and Pleasure than Duty and Honour . . .

Epicureanism and the devotional pursuit of pleasure in all its forms has been offered as an explanation for France's poor war effort. And it is a good one: a nation addicted to the finer things in life will always find war harder than a nation that is not. Unlike the English, the French do not thrive on privation. Madeleine says, 'I remember everyone around me as hungry and frightened. There was simply not enough to eat, and finding food took up most of people's time.' Her experience is echoed in Ophüls's documentary by the testimony of Pierre Mendès-France, politician and resistance fighter: 'It is very difficult to imagine what life was like then . . . There was *nothing* . . .

This was a country in which *everyone* spent their *whole* time looking for *everything*.'

Rationing in France, which was imposed by the enemy and did not (unlike British rationing) benefit from the people's consent, was very stringent. There was no tobacco, for example, a reality that British airmen tended to forget as they busily smoked their way through their hosts' hard-won cigarettes. Picture the Frenchman desperately trying to find the heroic Englishman his supply by digging out his stubs and rolling new ones with the remaining tobacco. Picture, too, the vast majority of the French population caught up in the business of searching for that lump of butter, or dash of cream, or that sliver of lard to flavour the fricassee or the ragout and supply that tiny drop of pleasure to the palate. The few who chose not to engage in this struggle against dearth hoisted themselves above reality, not with butter or cream or lard, but with *ideas* – of freedom, glory or solidarity – and joined the Resistance.

The precise nature of the idea being fought for varied, of course, and the Resistance movement reflected this diversity, for there was nothing monolithic about it. You could join *Libération* (CDLL) or the OCM (various shades of right) or the *Front National*, the *Franc-Tireur* (various shades of left) or *Combat* (which was somewhere in between). The regions of France tended to be dominated by one or other of these movements, and the ideology you were fighting for – communist, socialist, nationalist or Christian democrat – often depended on where you happened to be born. As the war went on, an attempt was made to amalgamate these various movements into efficient fighting units. This attempt gave rise to the AS (*Armée Secrète*), the MUR, the FTP and the MOI, most of which became, on the eve of the Allied landings, the FFI (*Force Française de l'Intérieure*). While de Gaulle was busy trying to overcome British scepticism and convince his hosts to put resources behind such a fragmented entity, a popular French song sung by Maurice Chevalier, 'Ça Fait d'Excellents Français', ridiculed the French Army for its mindless and debilitating sectarianism:

> *Le colonel était d'Action française,*
> *Le commandant était un modéré,*
> *Le capitaine était pour le diocèse,*
> *Et le lieutenant boulottait du curé.*
> *Le juteux était un fervent socialiste,*
> *Le sergent un extrémiste convaincu,*
> *Le caporal inscrit sur toutes les listes,*
> *Et l'deuxième class' au PMU.**

* 'The colonel was *Action Française*, / The major was a moderate, / The captain was for the diocese, / And the lieutenant was a rabid anti-cleric. / The adjutant was a fervent socialist, / The sergeant a hardened extremist, / The corporal was signed up to everything, / And the private was in the PMU.' *L'Action Française* is a right-wing anti-republican movement, founded in the early twentieth century. The PMU (*Pari Mutuel Urbain*) is France's monopolist bookmaker; its outlets are typically situated in bars, which have come to be referred to as PMUs by association.

France's defeat in June 1940 was swift and total. Contrary to the rumour put out at the time and broadly held to be true even today, France was not, militarily speaking, at a huge disadvantage. With Britain's help, she had more tanks and guns than the Germans. She had fewer planes and infantry than the enemy and her cavalry – left over from the First World War – still outnumbered her armoured divisions, but it was not the inferiority of her equipment that undid her. As de Gaulle's Resistance comrade Alain Peyrefitte put it, France was undone by the inferiority of her reasoning: 'Instead of grouping her tanks in armoured divisions, she littered them about at the disposal of her infantry, which didn't know how to use them. Instead of using her planes to defend the front, she let them fly about in the rear.' The French historian Marc Bloch, a veteran of the First World War who lived through the defeat of 1940, explained the rout of the French Army quite simply as the failure to face up to reality. Caught up in *ideas* of war that were largely outdated, her generals were unable to adapt to the reality of the speed of modern weaponry: the result was that they were simply outrun by the Wehrmacht.

The best illustration of the absurdity of French idealism in the context of war, however, is the story – told in *Le Chagrin et la Pitié* – of a group of bourgeois French housewives who decided to raise money to plant rose bushes along the Maginot Line in order to raise the spirits of the troops.

The famous Maginot Line, about which we used to

laugh in our history lessons as children, is frequently offered as a resounding metaphor for French pig-headedness, bureaucracy and idealism. This rampart, or rather 'line of firepower', 450 kilometres long, which cost the nation billions to create and which mobilised – or rather immobilised – thirty divisions, had been the pride of the French Army since its conception in the aftermath of the Treaty of Versailles. Animated by the spirit of 'Never Again', France's minister of war, André Maginot, was eager to believe his generals (Marshal Pétain being the most voluble among them) when they told him that the line would be impassable. When the wisdom of an entirely defensive strategy was contested in parliament as early as 1928, Maginot's characteristically French faith in the administration, in the specialists, but also crucially in the *idea*, was already discernible.

'The Border Commission and The Council of War have elaborated a plan. This plan has an advantage, that is that it exists,' he said simply.

Seven years later, when objections to this monolithic strategy were raised again, Maginot's successor, General Maurin, showed the same rigid adherence to an idea that had by now absorbed enormous funds.

'How can we still be considering an offensive strategy when we have spent billions on a defensive barrier?' he asked.

And that, it seems, was that. When the time came for the line to be put to the test and the Wehrmacht simply walked around it (taking the path through the Ardennes that they had taken in 1914), Clemenceau's joke that 'War is much too serious a matter to be entrusted to the military' had never been more pertinent.

Collaboration and Defeat

When Jack was nine months old, I went back to Oxford to finish my degree. At the end of the summer term, my grandmother came to stay with me in my digs. In the day, while she looked after Jack, I sat my finals. My grandmother kept me on a regime of chicken soup and bananas, the only thing I could eat without throwing up.

'With that kind of morning sickness', she told me, 'you must be having a girl.'

It turned out she was right. I was three months pregnant with Ella.

Every morning I put on my gown and cycled five minutes away to the examination halls on the High Street. Every morning I would stop, usually near the St Giles monument, and throw up on the pavement. After a few days, the invigilators kindly took the initiative of putting two dried biscuits on my desk to help me get through the exam without vomiting.

My finals over, I returned to Paris, to Laurent and *la bande* and my life as a bourgeois Parisian housewife. It was the summer of 1987. I would spend my days with Jack in Paris's various parks, all of them quite picturesque, with their topiary, their ordered flowerbeds and their gravel paths, and all quite unsuitable for children. Jack would play grubbily alongside the groomed Parisian children, while I sat, not with the mothers (they were all at work), but with the *au pair* girls on a bench and struggled through *Libération* – France's favourite left-wing daily newspaper; founded by Sartre and a group of eager Maoists in the early seventies, it was thriving back then but is now in steady decline. Haltingly and between waves of nausea, I read all about the trauma that was gripping the nation: the trial of Klaus Barbie in Lyon.

Klaus Barbie, the Butcher of Lyon, the personification of the barbarity of the Occupation, had been tracked down in Bolivia by French Nazi-hunter Serge Klarsfeld and brought back to stand trial for crimes against humanity in the very city where he had committed his atrocities. Six weeks of hearings over that long, hot summer of 1987, during which the whole of France was riveted to that stuffy, overcrowded courtroom in Lyon. Six weeks in which to face collectively – and for the first time – the true horror of what had gone on during *Les Années Noires* (the dark years).

For the first two days of the trial, over an eight-hour period, the president of the tribunal read out the catalogue of horrors attributed to the former Gestapo chief. Barbie sat in silence and listened. An unfortunate twist to his thin mouth gave the impression that the seventy-three-year-old Nazi was smiling.

At the end of his arraignment and to the horror of his victims, Barbie announced his decision not to attend the rest of the trial but to wait it out, as was his right, in the prison of Montluc, where he was being held and where he had once imprisoned the Jews and *résistants* he would deport to the camps.

In his absence, his victims, or their descendants, came to the bar one by one to bear witness to his crimes. As I read *Libération*'s vivid accounts of these tales of unspeakable suffering at the hand of a single man, I would repeatedly put down the paper – and breathe. The crimes that Barbie had committed against *résistant* fighters, which included the protracted torture of France's Resistance hero Jean Moulin, were considered war crimes and had lapsed. Only the crimes against Jews, which were considered crimes against humanity, have no statute of limitation. France's Jews, most of whom had been children at the time, were now standing up and speaking out about what they had suffered.

For the prosecution, Barbie's crimes were simply the manifestation of his merciless and gratuitous violence. For the defence, however, this old Nazi was being used as a scapegoat to preserve France from the discomfort of looking at a much harsher truth: the role she herself had played in these crimes. Barbie's lawyer, Jacques Vergès, believed it was time to examine that role.

Despite the best efforts of the president of the tribunal and the prosecution to stick to the crimes themselves, the trial, in the absence of the accused, became a kind of collective psychodrama in which France's history, or at least the current version of it, was being held up for scrutiny.

It gradually became clear that a large proportion of the crimes that were being described with such terrible clarity had been committed at the behest of French people. The raid on an orphanage at Izieu, for example – in which forty-four Jewish schoolchildren, tracked to a farmhouse east of Lyon, were arrested and sent to their deaths – had been organised after a tip-off from a neighbouring farm-worker, Lucien Bourdon. Many French people learnt, for the first time, that the deportation of Jewish children under sixteen had come about at the insistence of the French authorities themselves. Unprompted by the Germans, Prime Minister Laval had insisted that all children be deported with their families, probably in order to avoid scenes that might stir up public indignation. A telegram sent on 18 August 1942 to the French Ministry of the Interior and signed by René Bousquet, head of the French police in Vichy, testifies to the zeal with which the regime was prepared to help the Germans in their perse-cution of the Jews: 'Following my instructions of 5 August concerning operations for rounding up of Israelites . . .'

Henceforth, the telegram goes on, the old and infirm, visibly pregnant women, parents with children under two years old and all children under eighteen inside the 'Free Zone' would no longer be exempt from deportation. Bousquet then decided to include children under two years old, hitherto excluded from the convoys. Between 17 and 28 August 1942 three thousand children, many of whom were babies and toddlers, were taken by force from their parents inside the French internment camps and deported with adult strangers to the death camps. None of these children returned.

As Vergès took pains to point out, all of this was carried out with perfect efficiency by French civil servants and without the aid of men like Klaus Barbie. Vergès reminded the court that this efficiency would never have been possible without the groundwork of Vichy's anti-Semitic reforms. Two laws, passed on 3 October 1940 and 2 June 1941, laid down the 'Status of Jews' and set in motion their persecution. Henceforth all 'Israelites' of French or foreign nationality were required, by law, to have the word 'Jew' stamped on their identity cards. Vichy's indexing of three hundred thousand Jews made possible their exclusion from all the professions and paved the way for the mass arrests and deportations.

That summer I learnt – along with a generation of young French people – the full extent of France's involvement in the persecution of Europe's Jews. After the Barbie trial* and indeed the flurry of trials for crimes against humanity that followed – this time with Frenchmen in the dock – it was no longer possible to continue to preach mitigating circumstances for Vichy. Nor was it possible to go on perpetrating the myth of a massively resisting nation, nor the view of Marshal Pétain, head of the Vichy regime, as a well-meaning war hero playing a double game with the occupier.

Marshal Pétain and his rather more unpopular prime minister, Pierre Laval, managed to build a fascist regime in France under the auspices of the occupying forces. My

---

* Klaus Barbie was sentenced to life imprisonment on 341 charges. He died of cancer in 1991.

own children's history textbooks would still, in the mid-nineties, prefer to call Vichy 'authoritarian', specifying that the regime did not impose a one-party state and was therefore not technically 'fascist'. I noticed that school historians – as outlined in the *Manuel de Terminale* – carefully chose the word *unanimisme* instead of *totalitarisme* and described Vichy's ideology as 'reactionary, anti-liberal and anti-democratic' rather than fascist.

This semantic hair-splitting does not prevent these textbooks from acknowledging that Vichy was a police state, which ended up participating in the Final Solution. The textbooks also acknowledge the 'purifying zeal' with which Vichy mobilised the French population against the forces of *Anti-France*. Pétain's National Revolution declared war on its own citizens, who were held responsible for France's military defeat as well as her moral decline. Vichy's paramilitary police force (first the SOL or *Service d'Ordre Légionnaire* and then the *Milice* from 1943) would become right arm to the Gestapo. Its recruits sung an anthem in which they swore to

> *Faisons la France pure:*
> *Bolcheviks, francs-maçons ennemis*
> *Israël ignoble pourriture,*
> *Ecœurée, la France vous vomit.**

Knowing this, it was all the more intriguing to discover the strange inconsistencies within Vichy's reign of terror.

* 'Make France pure: / Bolsheviks, enemy freemasons, / Israel's vile scum, / Sickened, France vomits you up.'

Laval and Pétain, for a long time, stubbornly refused to give up French Jews to the Germans. Instead they made it their business to deliver any foreign Jews they could find, even if it meant dipping into the 'Free Zone'. After the infamous Wannsee Conference of January 1942, which gave birth to the Final Solution, Eichmann began to put pressure on Theodor Dannecker, head of the Gestapo in Paris, to deliver at least one hundred thousand Jews from France to the gas chambers. Dannecker, in turn, put pressure on Laval, who set about organising the biggest police raid on a religious community that Paris had ever seen. On 16 and 17 July 1942, nine thousand French policemen rounded up 13,152 men, women and children – Jews from Germany, Austria, Poland, Russia, Hungary and Czechoslovakia – and sent them to Drancy for deportation.

The Vel d'Hiv raid, as it came to be known (after the stadium where most of the families were held), was a turning point both for public opinion and for the French authorities. In its wake, the Germans tried to put pressure on Laval to denaturalise the seven thousand or so French Jews who had been given their nationality through a law passed in 1927. The Germans were increasingly infuriated by Laval's insolence and ingenuity in stalling the law's repeal* and were, from 1943 onwards, forced to carry out the arrest of French Jews without the help of the French police.

After Vel d'Hiv, protestations came from the heads of

* Report by Heinz Röthke to Helmut Knochen, SS-Standartenführer, 15 August 1943.

France's Christian community. The moving appeals, written by Cardinal Saliège in Toulouse and Cardinal Gerlier in Lyon, demanding an end to the inhuman treatment of the Jews, as well as the outcry of the head of the Protestant Church, Pastor Bœgner, helped to turn public opinion against Vichy. This shift, combined, no doubt, with the change in the fortunes of the Allied armies, made Laval give up doing the Gestapo's dirty work.

France has taken decades to face up to the truth about the Vichy regime. The French administration was filled after the war with technocrats who had served under Vichy. Many of them made fine careers. Some of them, including René Bousquet and Maurice Papon, were eventually indicted for crimes against humanity. Bousquet was shot by a lunatic before he could come to trial, and Papon was sentenced to ten years' imprisonment and released, due to ill health, after three – a decision that was widely criticised as pusillanimous.

François Mitterrand himself, who swore allegiance to Pétain, was honoured as late as 1943 with the *francisque* (Vichy's equivalent of the *Légion d'honneur*). He obstinately refused to apologise for Vichy's crimes and stuck to the casuistic argument that Vichy was an aberration in French history: an illegal regime, which had usurped the Republic. As he put it in 1992, 'The French nation was not involved in that, nor was the Republic.' In the end it was Chirac (only a child during the war) who, as soon as he came to power in 1995, stood up and apologised for France's role in the extermination of the Jews.

Over the past twenty years the business of facing the truth, with all its messy ambiguities, has helped France to recover from the trauma of the Occupation. It has also helped to reveal more positive inconsistencies, hitherto masked by France's habit of myth-making: the fact, as Serge Klarsfeld points out, that 240,000 people, three-quarters of France's Jewish population, survived the Shoah, 'thanks to the compassion and solidarity of countless French people'. When you consider that Serbia killed every last one of her Jews, and Poland, Estonia and Lithuania each slaughtered around 90 per cent of theirs, France – even with the complicity of Vichy – was one of the countries in Nazi-occupied Europe where the largest number of Jews survived. Despite Laval's ignoble initiative, 84 per cent of Jewish children were saved in France, the highest proportion in Europe.

France's incurable idealism makes her prone to extremes. She is a nation in thrall to the idea and, as such, highly vulnerable to its grubby relative, ideology. In spite of her best efforts, however – her fascist legions, her nationalism and her racist laws – France made a very poor working partner for the Nazis, who became increasingly exasperated by her inconsistencies. Hitler had always preferred the English to the French, whom he saw as immoral and racially impure. As General Walter Warlimont, of the Wehrmacht High Command, put it, 'For racial reasons Hitler seemed to prefer the English to the French. He had a view of France's decadence as something irreversible . . .'*

* Interviewed in *Le Chagrin et la Pitié*.

After the German invasion, André Gide, himself a Protestant, wrote in his diary: 'That puritan rigour by which Protestants, those spoilsports, often make themselves so hateful, those scruples of conscience, that integrity, that unshakeable punctuality, these are the things we have most lacked. Softness, surrender, relaxation in grace and ease, so many charming qualities that were to lead us, blindfolded, to defeat.'

10 Foreign Affairs

Cake and Spies

Young children in France are swept up by the State from an early age. You can put your toddler (provided that he or she is nappy-trained) into free, full-time education from the age of three, and in some cases two. For me, the temptation to hand my little ones over to the child-catcher that is *l'Education Nationale* was irresistible. By the time Jack was four and Ella nearly three, my days were free between eight-thirty and four. Sometimes, usually when my English or American girlfriends came to stay, I would feel guilty about my children's forced and premature socialisation.

On winter mornings, as I waved goodbye to them at the school gates when it was still dark outside and watched them disappear into a low, grey building, I would long to run after them and whisk them away to the adventure playground. Then I would remember, there are no adventure playgrounds, only tame, picturesque pony rides in the Luxembourg gardens. I would pick them up at four and my heart would melt at the sight of their little camp beds all in a row, on the pillow of each a cuddly toy – or, as the school Freudian would put it, *un objet de transfert* (transference object). The children would file out of the classroom in pairs, hand in hand, and fetch their coats from their peg in an orderly fashion. Then they would lay their coats on the ground in front of them, feed their little arms into the sleeves and, with an expert motion, flip their coats over their heads. They would only need help with the zip. All this impeccable regimentation made me wonder why the French had made such poor bedfellows for the Nazis.

While Jack was writhing and struggling in the mould and Ella settling comfortably into it, I began my working life. A friend from Oxford sent me off for an interview with the BBC Paris correspondent, Edward Stourton, who had just arrived from the Washington bureau and was looking for a researcher. Political correctness had not yet dawned in France and Edward seemed to welcome the respite from the new puritanism that was sweeping across America. A Roman Catholic himself, he had no difficulty slipping into French working rituals. He shared my view that there was little point in cutting short your lunch break when the whole of Paris only returned to their desks at three, nor was there much point in drinking water over lunch when your interviewee was drinking wine.

Many years later, even now that France has joined the global economy, French businessmen still take a proper lunch break and drink wine with their meal. Laurent and his colleagues, who work in investment banking, testify to the joy or suspicion shown by their English or American investors when they come to Paris on business.

They are surprised by the fact that while they invariably share a bottle of Bordeaux between three, their English guests will often get through a bottle each and the Americans will stick stubbornly to mineral water; to the French the relationship to alcohol seems, in both cases, somewhat excessive.

Shortly after I began working for the BBC Paris bureau, the French war criminal Paul Touvier was arrested in a monastery in Nice after forty-five years on the run. A devout Catholic and member of the *Milice*, Touvier had been hiding with his wife and two children in various monasteries across France ever since the war. The monks had pleaded 'right of asylum' as their reason for harbouring a man accused of crimes against humanity, and for some of them this was probably true, but for many it was clearly ideological compatibility that drove them. Anti-communism and anti-Judaism – strains that were still rife in the Catholic Church – made certain clerics take a lenient view of Touvier's crimes.

In those days (before John Birt and financial accountability) the BBC seemed to have endless resources. Documentaries were shot on very expensive 16mm film, generally by intense young men and women who dreamed of directing feature films. These films could take a year to make, from the research period (which might take six months) to editing and post-production. I remember having to find one hundred homing pigeons to provide a single shot for the Touvier film, a fifty-minute documentary made for Religious Programming that went massively over budget. This lavish approach meant that the researcher had plenty of time to go out and find the story. As a freelance researcher I was low down in the BBC pecking order, but working for 'Auntie' carried huge kudos in France, where her reputation for quality and impartiality opened many doors, some of which remained closed to French journalists. The stories I researched brought me into contact with the underbelly of French society, a world peopled with judges, politicians, delinquents, terrorists, cops and spies. Some of them became friends.

The eclectic friendships that I made during my years as a stringer for the British press stand as a measure of my incompetence as an investigative journalist. I now realise that by the time my career got under way, I had become irrevocably contaminated by the French cult of the *jardin secret*. Instead of proceeding as any self-respecting Anglo-Saxon reporter would do – by teasing the story from your source and then running with it – I found myself staying for coffee and cigars and listening to spooks, spies and investigative magistrates, for the sheer pleasure of learning. It became clear that with my menial status within the hierarchy of the BBC – and later, as a lowly stringer for the *Sunday Telegraph* – I could get away with filing anecdotal, 'colour' stories that hovered on the edge of a scoop, without ever betraying the implicit, though unstated request that my sources made of me to be discreet.

When the children were at school I would do my job –

which meant researching the stories that interested me (at the time, terrorism, espionage and organised crime) while keeping my employers in London happy but without blowing my contacts in France. Pusillanimous as this may sound to British journalists, this is very much the French approach to reporting. As everywhere else in French culture, the values of the press are fundamentally Catholic: take your pleasure – within the bounds of reason – and be discreet about it.

So it was that in my working life, I found myself constantly torn between my Anglo-Saxon impulse to find out the truth that lay behind things and a growing French tendency to keep it to myself.

Were I a true Brit, I told myself, my cosy evenings in a dining club in the sixteenth arrondissement with French counter-intelligence chiefs and their buddies from the French atomic agency would, by Monday morning, be on the front page of *The Times*. But then, I thought selfishly, they would never talk to me again. For these men and women, like all French people, love to talk. They cannot keep secrets. They have to flaunt their knowledge, their insights and their perspicacious overview. I would drink up their words and then go home to Laurent and sit up in bed with him and tell him all the things that I had learnt about his strange country – among them some of the reasons for her (as I saw it) rather contrary foreign policy.

I am sitting with Yves, retired head of French counter-intelligence, and his wife, Michelle, in their large, bright kitchen. The view is of a Normandy garden in winter: manicured lawn, poplars, Madame Bovary fog, limp but enduring roses.

Yves's wife cuts the *galette des rois*, a kind of almond cake that is eaten all over France in the first half of January. The *galette* testifies to the persistence of France's dual Roman and Catholic heritage. The Feast of the Kings, as it is known here, refers to the three kings from the Nativity story, but it is a Christian rehash of the rather more debauched, week-long festival of Saturnalia, during which, apart from going completely crazy, the Romans would send each other cakes. The French *galette* is made with very buttery, flaky or crusty pastry, depending on the region (here in Normandy it is flaky), and filled with a creamy frangipani.

Michelle cuts the cake into four large slices, one for each of us and one, as tradition dictates, for *le pauvre*, the vagrant who might show up at the door and need feeding. Hidden in one of the portions is a tiny porcelain figure known as *la fève*. It is either a religious symbol (the Black Madonna, one of the three kings) or a secular one (the Eiffel Tower, a sheep, a loaf of bread). The person who finds the *fève* in their slice becomes King (or Queen) and puts on one of the two gold paper crowns that the *boulanger* has provided with the cake.

'The tradition was banned during the Revolution as monarchistic,' Yves explains as I bite down on the *fève*.

'Well done!' Michelle exclaims. 'What is it?'

We all conclude that it is a shepherd.

'People took no notice of the ban of course,' Yves goes on. 'And in true French style, Napoleon authorised it again.'

'You have to choose your King,' Michelle says with a smile.

I put the paper crown on the ex-spymaster and we all dig in.

After tea, Yves and I and his new golden retriever, Voyou (Rogue – I presume as in State), move into the study. I want him to tell me about his insights and experiences, not because I haven't heard them before but because this time I wish to write them down.

Yves Bonnet, former head of the DST (*Direction de la Surveillance du Territoire*, French counter-intelligence), is a freethinker, a rare species in France. Protestant on both his mother's and father's side, he is, like many Huguenots, a passionate Anglophile, a sceptic and an iconoclast. Among his most recent ideas is a campaign to rehabilitate Pierre Cauchon, the collaborationist bishop who burnt Joan of Arc.

'He made a sensible decision,' he argues. 'The English would have done a much better job of ruling France than the imbeciles who came after that lunatic Charles VII. Just imagine, Lucy. With the Plantagenets at the helm, ruling Britain and France as one, what a great nation we would have made.'

As a spymaster operating towards the end of the Cold War, Yves says that he came to depend heavily on the

English. He refers to *La Six* (MI6) as 'still by far the best agency in the world'. Mistrustful of his sister house, the DGSE – which still, three decades after the *Rainbow Warrior* fiasco, drags around a reputation for incompetence – he quickly got into the habit of applying to the English for foreign intelligence.

'My external service is MI6,' he told a commission of inquiry investigating the lack of coordination between France's intelligence services. 'If I need to know anything, in China, in Pakistan, I'll call the English.'

'Do you know what you're saying?' the investigator asked him.

'Perfectly. If you want to work properly in this field, you work with the English.'

Yves recalls with satisfaction MI6's station chief in Paris, Kenneth Wright.

'With his perfect French, his *finesse* and his Cambridge-style distinction, the man seemed to have walked straight out of a John Le Carré novel.'

Yves notes that this was often the profile of agents working for *La Six*, which, as he puts it, employs a 'better calibre' than MI5. Despite his affection for the Secret Intelligence Service (SIS), Yves did work closely with MI5 on 'the Irish'.

'We went very far for the English over Ireland. We were MI5's annexe in Paris, intercepting arms for them, tapping phones. The Irish work took up thirty to forty French inspectors all year round, paid for by the Republic,' he adds. 'We're not a big agency so this was no small thing, but we were happy to do it.'

Ever since his time as head of the DST, Yves will not have a word said against British intelligence, which he believes offers 'in an imperfect world, a model of conduct, due to the simplicity of its structures, its coherence and its checks and balances'.

It must be said that Yves's experience of the United Kingdom dates back to the early eighties and was limited to his brief visits to The Travellers Club on Pall Mall, courtesy of Colin Figures, then head of MI6. When I mention some other, more contemporary aspects of British society, he stops me, as if reluctant to have his idyll marred.

'I know, I know. *Les Hooliganes*,' he says quaintly. 'It seems that in Britain the very best coexists beside the very worst. France does not have such contrasts. I suppose if I had to,' he concludes, euphemistically, 'I would choose the civilisation of the grape to that of the hop.'

A former Prefect and centre-right MP, Yves was nominated to head the DST by the socialist president François Mitterrand because he knew that this Protestant maverick would carry out vitally needed reforms to a sclerotic service without bowing to pressure from any faction. Yves remembers entering Mitterrand's study at the Elysée for the first time and discreetly craning his neck to see who was occupying the only photo frame on the president's desk. To his amusement and admiration it was not his wife, Danielle, or his daughter, Mazarine, but . . . Ronald Reagan.

Separated by their politics, Yves and his president were

united by a common mistrust of orthodoxy. Champion of the underdog, Yves's alliances are broad and eclectic. A friend, like Mitterrand, to the Serbs and the Iraqis, he has always fiercely opposed sanctions, which he calls 'the rich man's terrorism'. He has been a loyal friend to the Algerian military regime since their intelligence service (SM) helped him organise the release of Gilles Sydney Peyrolles, one of the first French hostages to be taken in Lebanon.* Yves has dined twice with Saddam Hussein, whom he described as 'logorrhoeic', and believes that Iran, a regime he despises, not only already has nuclear capability, but is perfectly entitled to it.

At this point, I tell Yves that I find it difficult to listen to him talking about geopolitics with that paper crown on his head.

Anti-Americanism and La Force de Frappe

'We are at war with America,' Mitterrand said in an interview with journalist Georges-Marc Benamou in 1995. 'A permanent war, a war without death. They are very hard, the Americans – they are voracious. They want undivided power over the world.'

This, as I would discover, is the conviction of a large number of French people, both young and old. Like many visceral antipathies, French anti-Americanism has its roots

---

* Gilles Sydney Peyrolles, kidnapped in Tripoli, northern Lebanon, on 23 March 1985. Between April and October 1985 four hostages – Nicolas Kluiters, Dennis Hill, Arkadi Katkov and William Buckley – would be murdered by their kidnappers in Lebanon.

in history. When I detected it, even in my own children, I became eager to understand its origins.

The week the British and Americans declared war on Iraq, I went to see Yves. I knew that he would provide a useful perspective on this new breach between France and the Anglo-Saxon world. We sat in his flat near the Eiffel Tower, surrounded by his wife's luminous oil paintings and a posse of Scottish terriers. His response was more laconic than I had expected.

'I'm afraid that all they are doing is taking the noose from around Iran's neck,' he said. 'With the Sunni regime destroyed, the mullahs will simply have a huge playground in which to extend their Islamic Revolution.'

A man of the Cold War, Yves has little patience with the politics of interference inaugurated by Clinton (or rather, rehabilitated by him), drooled over by Blair and harnessed, most successfully, by G. W. Bush. For people like Yves, better the dictator you know.

'The only thing that surprises me in all this', he went on, 'is the attitude of the English. Americans can be forgiven for their ignorance but the British have a sense of History. They *know* the region. Surely they can foresee the chaos that is to come.'

I relayed the theory that I had read in the editorial of a major British broadsheet, that Blair hoped to control Bush, act as a kind of moderator once in the theatre.

Yves said he thought this sounded like vainglory.

'I do not think this invasion makes sense but I will say one thing,' he said. 'France has behaved very badly.'

Did he not think that Dominique de Villepin's speech to the UN was rather magnificent?

'Magnificent and ridiculous,' he replied. 'That is what we French do best: hover between the sublime and the absurd. But that is not what I am talking about. I am referring to Chirac's behaviour. Giving the impression that he is working with his English allies to find a diplomatic solution, then at the last minute threatening to use his veto. How embarrassing for Blair. It is unacceptable. I will go further, I believe it was Chirac's shabby manoeuvre that finally drove Blair into Bush's arms.'

Few French men or women took Yves's rigorous position on their country's pre-war diplomacy. Most did not see beyond the simple fact that their leaders had been right not to involve them in a dubious and protracted conflict that has left the world a good deal less safe. I realise that the fact that the French may have been right about Iraq does not endear her to most Britons and Americans – in spite of the fact that the war has become increasingly unpopular in both countries.

When I asked Yves why he was so forgiving of the British and so tough on the Americans, he answered: 'If you asked that question to anyone in the French intelligence community, their answer would be the same: history.'

When Yves became head of French counter-intelligence he discovered a deeply Anglophile environment in which anti-American sentiment was not only permitted but encouraged. The American secret service is seen as big and cumbersome, with more money than sense.

'The Americans are overly reliant on technical intelligence,' he told me. 'And the standard of their analysis is very poor. The CIA is an enormous machine which produces very meagre results.'

And yet Yves is more generous than many inside the 'Ring of Secrecy' for whom the CIA's blunders have seriously endangered the West, the most disastrous of which is nowadays held to be Peshawar* and the ensuing rise of Islamic militancy.

With regard to the intelligence pointing to Iraq's so-called weapons of mass destruction, Yves, who has remained friends with Sir Richard Dearlove,† beleaguered head of MI6 at the time of the invasion, insists – memos and reports notwithstanding – that MI6 was not at fault.

'It was simply not possible that British intelligence would ever make a mistake of that magnitude,' he said.

Far beyond any particular grievance, however, French anti-Americanism appears to stem from a deep cultural incompatibility. Like de Gaulle, Yves and his kind con-

---

* Peshawar in northern Pakistan was a military training camp for the Mujahideen financed by the CIA as part of its war against the Soviets in Afghanistan.

† Minutes of the prime minister's meeting on Iraq, Downing Street, 23 July 2002: 'C (Richard Dearlove) reported on his recent talks in Washington. There was a perceptible shift in attitude. Military action was now seen as inevitable. Bush wanted to remove Saddam through military action, justified by the conjunction of terrorism and WMD. But the intelligence and facts were being fixed around the policy.'

sider the Americans as uncultured and unsubtle, vices that for the French are unforgivable.

This disdain for the Americans and admiration for the British makes Yves particularly sensitive to what he sees as Britain's servitude to US interests. He, like many French people, was excited by the prospect of Tony Blair governing Britain. A French-speaker with a home in France, he would surely turn towards Europe, perhaps even offer France a welcome alternative to her rather uncomfortable partnership with Germany.

If Blair's fantasy, on taking office, was to build a foreign policy that would bestride both Europe and America, he soon recanted. His decision to ride shotgun with Bush into war with Iraq put an end to any possibility of a bipartite policy. Agreeing with Nelson Mandela's remark that Blair was 'the foreign minister of the United States', it is Yves's understanding that all of history since the First World War has led ineluctably to this rather unsatisfactory role for Britain. And like many Frenchmen of his generation, he watches from the sidelines, clutching his head in despair.

Yves's analysis, shared by many French people, is that the US has a history of conning Europe, often with an accompanying naivety that only makes the sting more humiliating. In 1919, President Woodrow Wilson arrived at the Paris Peace Conference brandishing the idealism of a young nation just starting to flex its muscles. He presented his 'fourteen points' for peace to the imperial powers of Britain and France, represented by two old men, Lloyd

George and Georges Clemenceau. Neither Clemenceau – whose nation had lost more than one and a half million souls – nor Lloyd George – who had lost almost a million – liked Wilson's plan, which, as they saw it, left them insufficiently compensated for their losses and still exposed to further aggression. Neither of them appreciated being lectured on the evils of colonialism by a nation that was emerging as the world's new and indeed only economic superpower. The principal difference in the positions of these two old men was that Lloyd George was cannier in disguising his distaste than his fiery French counterpart, who, despite having lived in America and been married to an American woman, stubbornly refused to speak anything to Woodrow Wilson but French.

What is certain is that Wilson irritated both men. Sigmund Freud, in his rather strange collaborative biography of the American president, *Woodrow Wilson: A Psychological Study*, also confessed to have been irritated by his subject: 'His career from 1876 at Princeton to the day he was received in Paris as the Saviour of Mankind offers a remarkable example of the power of the Super-Ego to drive to success a man of weak body and neurotic constitution.'

This home-schooled son of an overbearing Presbyterian preacher did not learn to read until he was twelve – an idea that would have shocked the French. He had then spent the rest of his life trying to prove himself to his father. His apparently contradictory policies (towards both war and peace) were, Freud argued, born of an inner conflict between a heady and aggressive urge to contest the internalised father figure (by going to war) and the desire to placate it (by playing the Prince of Peace). Freud's reading might equally apply to another cowed son, who would also decide to play global *gendarme* but for much higher stakes.

At the time of the Treaty of Versailles, Woodrow Wilson was extremely popular with the peoples of Europe, who were exhausted and traumatised by the war. Both Clemenceau and Lloyd George, however, saw the American president as an ingénue, whose idealism masked – perhaps even to himself – a dangerous will to power. Wilson's decision to send his peace terms directly to the Germans without first consulting his French and British allies was to them a clear sign of his sense of entitlement.

From a French perspective Britain, in spite of her vanished empire and her weak economy, was, by virtue of her role in the Second World War, firmly in the victors' camp and as such entitled to aspire to a certain status in the world.

'Britain won that war,' Yves says. 'Or at least enabled us not to lose it. The Americans entered late because they had no choice. In the end, Britain was the nation that paid most dearly for US involvement. She sacrificed her independence.'

After Hiroshima, it was clear that nuclear capability held the key to status and independence in the world. Notwithstanding his legendary differences with his British hosts, de Gaulle strongly admired British culture and disliked America. He was deeply mistrustful when he saw the United States trying, as he saw it, to lock down the nuclear industry. In 1953 the general would have heard President Dwight Eisenhower's rallying 'Atoms for Peace' speech to the UN and reminded himself that the road to Hell is paved with good intentions.

'It is with the book of history,' said Eisenhower, 'and not with isolated pages, that the United States will ever wish to be identified. My country wants to be constructive, not destructive. It wants agreement, not wars, among nations. It wants itself to live in freedom, and in the confidence that the people of every other nation enjoy equally the right of choosing their own way of life.'

Eisenhower's 'Atoms for Peace' programme was, ostensibly, a plan to supply friendly nations (which at the time included Iran and China) with atomic materials and technology, to be used to civilian ends.

'To the making of these fateful decisions, the United States pledges before you – and therefore before the world – its determination to help solve the fearful atomic dilemma, to devote its entire heart and mind to find the way by which the miraculous inventiveness of man shall not be dedicated to his death, but consecrated to his life.'

Eisenhower's offer carried with it the right of the United States to verify that the transferred materials were being used for peaceful purposes. Any nation joining the programme would therefore have to relinquish nuclear military independence, an idea that would have been unacceptable to de Gaulle. He interpreted Eisenhower's

'Atoms for Peace' initiative as the vehicle through which an already dominant America would organise and control the world nuclear market.

If Eisenhower's intention was peaceful, the result of his 'Atoms for Peace' programme was an opening up, to other participants, of the arms race (atoms for peace, through reprocessing and plutonium extraction, can quite easily become atoms for war). It also led to an increase in the tempo of the race and a hardening of the Soviet resolve. Eisenhower's focus on the peaceful uses of atomic energy, hugely popular with US and international public opinion, in the end worked to camouflage his own administration's rapid build-up of atomic weaponry.

For this reason, de Gaulle, who had returned to power in 1958, would watch with suspicion as President Kennedy and Harold Macmillan, nearly a decade later, went into negotiations on the matter of nuclear interdependency.

The Nassau Agreement signed in December 1962 between Kennedy and Macmillan was proof to de Gaulle that he had been right to distrust the Americans. As far as he was concerned, the agreement simply swindled the British out of their nuclear independence. De Gaulle's reading of Nassau is highly questionable but it does offer an insight into the French perspective, which as events would show, still dictates much of her foreign policy.

Back in March 1960, Harold Macmillan had left a meeting at Camp David with Eisenhower, confident that Britain had secured an independent nuclear capability. In a secret quid pro quo deal, Macmillan offered Eisenhower the use of Holy Loch, Scotland, as a base for America's Polaris missile submarines, in exchange for which Britain would receive delivery, as soon as it was ready, of the weapon then being developed by the US Airforce. This was not a bomb, but a nuclear air-to-ground missile called Skybolt. Skybolt could be used in conjunction with British Vulcan bombers to penetrate Soviet airspace. After the Camp David meeting, a joint project office was set up between the RAF and the US Airforce to develop the weapon.

The following year, when Kennedy came to power, he met a barrage of resistance to the Skybolt programme. His secretary of defence, Robert McNamara, headed the campaign. McNamara criticised the whole idea of Skybolt, judging that 'limited nuclear capabilities, operating independently, are dangerous, expensive, prone to obsolescence and lacking in credibility as a deterrent'.* In the same speech McNamara rejected the notion of small nations like Britain even possessing an independent nuclear deterrent: 'In particular, relatively weak national nuclear forces with enemy cities as their targets are not likely to be sufficient to perform even the function of deterrence.'

Less than two weeks before Kennedy's talks with Macmillan in Nassau, the former secretary of state Dean Acheson gave a speech to a group of students at West Point that was – and probably still is – a pretty accurate

* Robert S. McNamara, 'Defense Arrangements of the North Atlantic Community', *Department of State Bulletin* 47 (9 July 1962).

summary of the American view: 'Great Britain has lost an empire and has not yet found a role. The attempt to play a separate power role, that is, a role apart from Europe, a role based primarily on a "special relationship" with the United States, a role based on being head of the Commonwealth [is] about played out.'

By the time he came to the negotiating table, Harold Macmillan must have been smarting with wounded pride. He already knew that Kennedy had decided to scrap Skybolt. Britain – who had cancelled 'Blue Streak', her own ballistic missile programme – had been left high and dry by the Americans.

Kennedy and Macmillan talked for three days. By the time they emerged, blinking, into the Caribbean sunshine, Kennedy had agreed to provide Britain with the far more advanced, second-generation Polaris missiles instead of Skybolt. In exchange, Britain would honour her commitment to provide the Americans with a strategic base at Holy Loch, Scotland.

De Gaulle, who had received Macmillan at Rambouillet two days before his trip to the Bahamas, had hoped to engage him in a nuclear partnership with France. In his eyes, the only impediment to this would be Britain's continued nuclear alliance with America. After all, the goals of these two old men, at the head of two defunct empires, were the same – to claw back some prestige and independence in the world – and, as they both knew, only nuclear fire could do that.

After the Rambouillet meeting, de Gaulle told his

secretary of state, Alain Peyrefitte, 'England's back is broken,' an impression that was only confirmed five days later, when Macmillan left Nassau. De Gaulle did not see the Anglo-American agreement as a victory for Macmillan, who had rather brilliantly steered Kennedy round to offering the Polaris missiles. As far as de Gaulle was concerned, the fact that Polaris offered a better defence for Britain than Skybolt, and at a very low financial cost, was irrelevant. He thought first as a soldier, then as a politician. As soon as the British accepted Polaris, the RAF would lose its strategic-deterrent role* and, for de Gaulle, this was an unacceptable price for a sovereign nation.

It is impossible to understand French foreign policy – which so often appears just contrary and intractable – without understanding her particular role in nuclear history. Indeed, French national pride has become inextricably linked to her perceived independence in the world – an independence to which, without her nuclear might, she could have had no pretension.

Even after her humbling defeat in the Second World War, France – whose scientists had, before the war, put her at the head of the atomic race – would never give up her ambition for nuclear self-sufficiency. On 18 October 1945, almost a year before the Americans created their Atomic Energy Commission, de Gaulle set up the *Commissariat à l'Energie Atomique* (CEA), nominating as

* The submarine-launched Polaris missile became operational on 1 July 1967.

its director the physicist Frédéric Joliot-Curie, who, with his wife, Irene, had won the Nobel Prize for their work on artificial radiation and nuclear fission. The fact that Joliot-Curie was a card-carrying communist would not endear him to the Western world's scientific community, but it did not deter de Gaulle. He shelved his mistrust of communists, for Joliot-Curie had proven his credentials. In 1939 he had the insight to order 6 tons of uranium oxide from the Belgian Congo and nearly all of the available heavy water from Norway, and send them to England for safekeeping.

From 1945 onwards, de Gaulle's nuclear policy was backed by a broad political consensus. Despite the widely held view that the general drove France's nuclear programme single-handedly with the sheer force of his obsession for sovereignty, all parties within the volatile Fourth Republic (with the notable exception of the pro-Soviet Communist Party) stood firmly behind the nuclear programme. This explains why it advanced apace even while the general was not in power. It gathered momentum after the humiliation of Suez, when the victorious advance of the British–French–Israeli expeditionary force was brought to an abrupt halt by the Soviet threat of a nuclear missile attack. In a note to Prime Minister Anthony Eden, Soviet Premier Nikolai Bulganin had warned: 'If this war is not stopped, it carries the danger of turning into a Third World War.'

After the wake-up call of Suez, both Britain and France understood the necessity of owning a convincing nuclear capability if they were to play any significant role on the world stage. To this end, Britain turned to America, paving the way for the Nassau Agreement, while France resolved that, as soon as she could, she would end any reliance on the superpower for her foreign policy – a decision that would lead to her gradual but ineluctable withdrawal from NATO in July 1966.

Of his nation's remarkable feat of acquiring total nuclear independence, de Gaulle said, 'We owe nothing to the Americans except trip-ups.'

This was, of course, not fair. As Yves would explain to me that afternoon over tea, de Gaulle had a lot to thank the Americans for, though he could not admit this publicly. One of his key military advisers, a former RAF pilot called Pierre-Marie Gallois, had, as far back as April 1956, brought de Gaulle about 20 kilos' worth of NATO files containing all the details of the US military's strategy of 'massive retaliation'. These files – which de Gaulle helped Gallois carry to the lift when the briefing ended in the early hours of the morning – were brought to him at the suggestion of the deputy Supreme Allied Commander Allied Forces Europe, General Lauris Norstad, a man at the time sympathetic to the French position. Norstad came to regret his decision to share this precious information when it became clear that France's goal was to set up an independent nuclear force at odds with both NATO strategy and American interests.

Listening to Yves on the subject of Cold War nuclear proliferation, the apparently contrary nature of French policy makes perfect sense. The historian Linda Colley, in her brilliant study of British nationhood, *Britons: Forging the Nation*, observed that the countries making up the United Kingdom – formed at the beginning of the eighteenth century – managed largely to find their sense of national unity by rallying around their hostility towards the French. I have always been struck by the fact that the French do not return this hostility. Where anti-British sentiment does occur in France, it seems feeble in comparison (stemming, perhaps, from some unhappy romantic experience on an exchange trip to Brighton, or from an unpleasant encounter with a football supporter on the loose in France during the World Cup). It does not have the depth or conviction of manufactured mythology, like the British hatred of the French, still dutifully upheld by the tabloids. If one had to find an equivalent cultural antagonism in France, it would have to be towards the Americans.

'America is the only nation in history which miraculously has gone directly from barbarism to degeneration without the usual interval of civilisation,' said Georges Clemenceau. This savage remark reflects the nature of French anti-American sentiment, even today. Yves's comments about American ignorance of History betray a similar prejudice.

Intellectual snobbery lies at the heart of the French sense of self. Her education system, her so-called meritocracy – based not on birth or money but on academic achievement – indeed her whole society is constructed around rationalist principles that many French people believe are the opposite of American values. As most French people see it, France is secular, while America is religious. France values Learning and Culture, while America values Power and Money.

After May '68, American capitalism became the target of a generation of French intellectuals. Since then, anti-American sentiment has so infused France's mainstream press that no one seems to notice it any more. It reached its apogee in September 2001, when a series of editorials, after offering the requisite condolences, went on to argue that America had deserved the attacks on the World Trade Center, or at least, had it coming to her. Jean-Marie Colombani, chief writer and publisher of *Le Monde*, wrote a piece on the day after the attacks entitled 'We are all Americans'.* The analysis that followed was rather more equivocal in its support than the title.

'The reality is, surely, that of a world without counter-powers, physically destabilised and dangerous, as a result, in the absence of any multi-polar equilibrium. And America, alone in her power, in her hyperpower . . . has ceased to draw the peoples of the globe to her; or, more exactly, in certain parts of the globe, she seems no longer to attract anything but hatred . . . And perhaps even we ourselves in Europe, from the Gulf War to the use of F16s against Palestinians by the Israeli Army, have underestimated the hatred which – from the outskirts of Jakarta to

* 12 September 2001.

Durban, via the rejoicing crowds of Nablus and of Cairo – is focused on the United States . . . Couldn't it be, then, that America gave birth to this devil?'

Nowadays, French anti-American sentiment is expressed through the more covert form of anti-globalisation. This includes a resistance to unbridled capitalism, a defence of regional (as opposed to national) identity, but also a championing of all peoples or nations perceived to be victims of oppression. It also seems, quite often, to act as political camouflage for anti-Israeli sentiment (embedded within Colombani's critique of America is an attack on her support for Israel). This position can, in some cases, spill over into an expression of anti-Semitism.

As my own small experiences with Nathalie and *la bande* had already shown me, the anatomy of French anti-Semitism is varied and complex. You will find it in the oddest places. José Bové, hero of the French anti-globalisation movement *La Fédération Paysanne*, moustachioed cheese-maker, champion of cultural diversity and GM vandal, managed to get himself arrested while on a trip to Israel. On his return he suggested in an interview on French TV that Mossad was behind the recent wave of attacks against French synagogues.

'Who profits from the crime? The Israeli government and its secret services have an interest in creating a certain psychosis, in making believe that there is a climate of anti-Semitism in France, in order to distract attention from what they are doing.'

Anti-Semitism seems impossible to wipe out in France.

It shifts and mutates, changing shape with each new generation. Today, it can be found lying just below the surface of Bové's otherwise quite legitimate struggle against cultural hegemony. It can also be found lurking beneath the widespread contempt for the current president.

Nicolas Sarkozy talks without difficulty about his father's Hungarian origins, frequently referring to himself as the son of an immigrant. He never, on the other hand, invokes his mother's Jewish roots, as if to do so in a nation whose anti-Semitism is ever-present and unresolved would be too risky.

During a visit to one of France's rioting suburbs (euphemistically referred to by the press and by politicians as 'difficult') Sarkozy was, as usual, bombarded with abuse from angry youths, many of whom were Muslims of North African origin. The French TV crew covering the incident failed to report the exact wording of their abuse. France's fifth channel, France 5, claiming poor sound quality, chose to subtitle the real chant, 'Sarkozy, Filthy Jew!' as 'Sarkozy, Fascist!'

That a TV editor would run the risk of making an edit so politically loaded and so clearly tendentious is as baffling as the strange *omertà* that seems to surround Sarkozy's Jewish heritage. The media clearly plays a continuing role in upholding the myth of France as a liberal, enlightened and tolerant nation. I have often met with incomprehension or resentment when I have compared France's immigrant suburbs to America's black and Hispanic ghettos. Still obsessed with the idea of equality through rapid integration, France will not own up to the seriousness of the problems she is facing in these non-ghettos of hers.

Traumatised by the history of her own intolerance, France takes cover behind the myths inaugurated by her Revolution. In the name of equality, it remains unacceptable in France to refer to the Jewish or Muslim or Arab component of a person's identity. The message is: we are all equal by virtue of the fact that we are all French. (Some, however, are clearly more French than others.)

Even my own children baulked when I asked them if any of their friends were Muslim.

'What kind of a question is that, Mum?'

For them, my question was politically suspect. I could not convince them that it is only when a culture or a religion is regarded as intrinsically inferior that it becomes taboo to mention it.

It is interesting to note that Sarkozy's enemies, unwilling to refer to his Jewish roots, refer instead to his partiality to America. Hence the rather limp and bizarre insult frequently used against Sarkozy – '*Sarko, l'Américain*'. The subliminal message underlying this label is not only that the president is pro-Israel (and therefore deaf to the plight of the Palestinians and, by extension, all Arabs), but also quintessentially *un-French*. Like de Gaulle before them, many French people consider America to be a kind of anti-model. If called upon to find a country whose values are most opposed to their own, most of the French people I have met would not say Cuba or Burma or North Korea or even England. At the top of their list would be the United States of America.

Of the United States, Hubert Vedrine, former socialist foreign minister in the Mitterrand government, said: 'The first characteristic of America, which explains her foreign policy, is that she has considered herself since her birth as a chosen nation whose role is to enlighten the rest of the world.'

The most striking thing about this remark is that it could so easily be applied to France. Indeed it seems that most French anti-American sentiment stems from rivalry between two cultures that are not embarrassed to offer universal moral lessons. Both nations consider themselves the first democracies. France never misses an opportunity to describe herself, particularly in international politics, as 'the nation of human rights', while America has no qualms about naming a military offensive 'Operation Enduring Freedom'.

By favourably comparing the British to the Americans in their understanding of the past, my good friend Yves was referring to the Britain that he encountered as a spy back in the eighties. This was a society – or the vestiges of a society – that no longer exists. Since Margaret Thatcher's quiet revolution, Britain has moved closer and closer to America and her total and unswerving commitment to consumerism. One of the consequences of this choice has been the effect it has had on our sense of history.

When Blair finished what Thatcher had started and rid the nation of the taboo surrounding the making of

money,* he paved the way for a society that lives in a perpetual present, turned towards a near and endlessly allur-
ing future. Reflected and glorified by our mass media, this
peripatetic motion towards commercial gratification
blocks out the past and makes it irrelevant. The annoy-
ingly prophetic Alexis de Tocqueville's observations of
nineteenth-century America could quite easily apply to
contemporary Britain: '[They] cleave to the things of this
world as if assured that they will never die, and yet are in
such a rush to snatch any that come within their reach, as
if expecting to stop living before they have relished them.
They clutch everything but hold nothing fast, and so lose
grip as they hurry after some new delight.'

In clinging to an archaic, quasi-socialist cultural model,
France has not fully embraced consumerism. It is still difficult, despite President Sarkozy's personal wish to be able to
go shopping on a Sunday, to find a shop open in France on
the Lord's Day, or even at lunchtime. In Paris, as well as
the provinces, most local shops close between one and
three or four in the afternoon. The French still feel either
guilty or slightly bored about the business of accumulating
money. They still believe that the accumulation of knowledge affords greater status than wealth. Debt is widely perceived as a little sinful. France's very backward banking
system has never really come round to credit. Even before
the 2008 credit crunch it was always very difficult to get a
bank loan in France. Overdrafts are strongly discouraged,

* 'We are extremely relaxed about people getting filthy rich.' Peter
Mandelson on New Labour, *Financial Times*, 23 October 1998.

and to qualify for a mortgage buyers must prove that their annual income covers their debt three times over. Never having fully embraced the concept of personal loans (only the State, like the monarchy before it, is allowed to get into debt), France, whose budget deficit has dropped since the crash, below that of Britain,* now finds herself surprisingly buoyant in the current storm.

In spite of all of Sarkozy's efforts to show them the way, however, the French make poor consumers. Not enough of them read newspapers and so the media cannot gain enough traction to attract the advertising to feed the machine. They do not get into debt and so they tend, in a very old-fashioned way, to buy what they need. In this kind of environment all-out consumerism cannot thrive.

In this relatively slow and archaic society, History is still relevant, even to the young. Ask a French teenager what they think of when they think of the Second World War and you will get a fairly clear answer. They will probably mention the persecution of the Jews, Marshal Pétain, German soldiers on the streets. Some of them will invoke a great-uncle who joined the *maquis*, for family stories of collaboration are less likely to have been passed down than Resistance stories.

Ask the same question to a British teenager and his or her references will probably come from television docu-dramas or American cinema (*Saving Private Ryan*, *Pearl Harbor*, *Schindler's List*).

As one English secondary-school teacher of history

---

* The IMF forecasts the French budget deficit for 2009 at 5.5 per cent, compared with 7.2 per cent for Britain and 12 per cent for the US.

explained to me, 'History has to be dumbed down and glamorised a little for British kids. A fifteen-year-old's perception of the Second World War would be unlikely to involve family links or be personalised in any way, but rather focused on Hitler and the Holocaust – celebrity and scandal.' In a culture dedicated to *the next thing* – the next film, the next handbag, the next holiday, the next mortgage payment – there is no room for the past. Put simply, France still has *time* for History.

Perhaps the reason for Blair's baffling foreign policy decisions can be found here. Perhaps when it was time to weigh up History (in this case, his own nation's memory of her experiences in the Middle East) against the Here and Now of American capitalism (with the shimmering mirage of oil concessions), Blair was simply dazzled. This would explain the complete loss of his faculties when in the presence of the former leader of the free world. The conversation that immortalised Britain's vassalage to America, recorded during the G8 conference in St Petersburg in July 2006, when both parties thought that the microphones were switched off, can still be heard on YouTube. Imagine the scene: Bush seated, popping food into his mouth and chewing loudly like some bored monarch, while Blair stands over him, stammering his diplomatic suggestions, all of which are ignored. The French took no pleasure from the spectacle. From my experience, people were shocked. For to them, British dependency on America only heralds France's own inevitable submission to the dominant model.

11 Tolérance Zéro

Cops and Spooks

In the summer of 1993, when my children were six and eight years old, I went to the building of France's secret police force, *Les Renseignements Généraux* (RG), on the rue des Saussaies, a tortuous, narrow street only a stone's throw from the Elysée Palace. As part of my research for the BBC, I was to meet the officers in charge of domestic anti-terrorism, which, at the time, divided most of its attention between the Corsican (FLNC) and the Basque separatists (ETA). As I would soon discover, the section devoted to the eradication of political violence on Corsica was peopled, to a large extent, by Corsicans. These men (there were no women in this particular department at the time) were devout Jacobins, hard-core defenders of the unity of the French Republic, self-confessed Napoleon-lovers and devotees of the doctrine of the ends justifying the means. They all wore the obligatory French plain-clothesman's leather *blouson* jacket and carried their Smith & Wessons in holsters around their ankles.

I was researching a documentary on the Basque armed group ETA, for which the *Renseignements Généraux* had agreed to give me an off-the-record briefing. As it turned out, the three men who received me on the fifth floor had already 'met' me. I had been filmed at the flat of the Paris representative of the then entirely legal Basque political party *Herri Batasuna* (outlawed by the Aznar government in 2003). The first thing the three undercover policemen expressed on greeting me was their disappointment that I was wearing trousers. They then decided to explain that they had me on film wearing a skirt and that they all felt a skirt became me better. Ten minutes of banter followed in which the three of them discussed the erotic tastes of the Basque militant whom they had under surveillance, after which they all decided that I was probably not his type anyway.

After this, it was difficult for me to believe that any of them were capable of providing any insight into my subject at all. I was, as it turned out, not wrong. Any information that I received from the RG over the years, on any story, had to be treated with the utmost suspicion. It became apparent that they always had an agenda, a message to convey to the terrorist organisation they were working on or to the public at large; they had no interest whatsoever in diffusing the truth. Their buffoonery that day dissembled a ruthless efficacy. One of these three men was a Corsican named Bernard Squarcini, who would eventually be nominated by President Sarkozy as head of Yves' old service, the DST. Squarcini – or Squarsh, as he is affectionately known by his fellow officers – has the reputation of a quiet man, efficient, hard-working and extremely loyal to Sarkozy. Since he was given the task of uniting two forces that have always despised each other (the RG and the DST), he would need all of these qualities.

The *Renseignements Généraux* was the administrative baby of Vichy's infamous *Milice*. Until 1 July 2008 it was the only remaining secret and political police force in a Western democracy. The RG took its orders from the minister of the interior and, unlike the *Gendarmerie* or the *Police Nationale*, its employees were not allowed to carry out arrests. They therefore earned the reputation of goalhangers, often attaching themselves to key investigations at the last minute in order to steal some of the glory of the arrest. To the 'noble' forces like the *Gendarmerie* and the *Police Judiciaire* (PJ), RG employees were not really policemen but spooks or *barbouzes*.

Benefiting from an extensive network of employees and informers, the RG had units (*effectifs*) in even the remotest areas of the Republic. Until recently the provincial units of the RG were operated by men and women, some of whom were required to keep their job secret. These people were expected, in exchange for their salary, to file reports on certain members of the community deemed to be of interest to the government. In the past this meant communists, unionists and indeed any leftwing activist. It might also include neo-Nazis and skinheads, anyone who might be considered potentially subversive. But, as one employee of French counterintelligence put it to me, 'These people were paid per sheet of paper blackened. You couldn't stop them. They were simply spying on their neighbours, reporting on the extra-marital activities of the local company executive. It became utterly ridiculous.'

As late as 2004, the RG was responsible for gathering information for the government on voting patterns, making their own rather dubious predictions at each election. Although it became increasingly clear that this force was an embarrassment to any self-respecting democracy, the RG's resources proved so invaluable to each successive government that it would quickly drop any pre-electoral pledge to dismantle it. This situation helped to fashion a police force unlike any other and probably contributed to the air of nonchalance and swaggering entitlement common to most RG employees I met.

It has been my experience that the urban French policeman (not the *gendarme*, who operates in the provinces and, as part of the military, has a more disci-plined ethos) is a breed apart. Living in a patriarchal bub-ble, thriving on camaraderie and adrenalin, the French policeman and even his female counterpart (who has to embrace the archaisms if she wants to survive) is fre-quently sexist and racist with perfect impunity. Even offi-cers of North African or French Caribbean origin feel they must join in with the kind of banter that would make *The Sweeney* seem politically correct by comparison. No mat-ter how hard French television tries to reconfigure this stereotype by pumping out series inspired and even copied from British and American TV, this reality persists on the ground and there seems little sign that things will change any time soon, particularly given President Sarkozy's special fondness for the police, who have reciprocated his love in large measure.

The serious consequence of all this is the climate of immunity that has long surrounded police brutality in France. When it does occur, it is invariably towards suburban youths of immigrant origin, and even if the incident sparks off a riot lasting for several weeks, it is unlikely ever to come to trial. All through the eighties, in suburbs like Vaulx-en-Velin to the east of Lyon, the police shot or beat youths of Arab origin and got away with it. In 1982 three people – Wahid Hachichi, Ahmed Bouteija and Mohamed Abidou – were shot dead in the Lyonnais suburbs by local police. By mid-1987 three more youths had been killed. In each case, the officer responsible was either transferred or acquitted.*

By 1990, all it took for Vaulx-en-Velin to explode was a fatal accident involving a police car and two kids on a moped. The nation watched the ensuing uprisings on their TV sets, wondering why all this rage when Mitterrand's urban rehabilitation programme had thrown so much money at Lyon's high-rise suburbs.

'Why would a renovated district, one that we were led to believe was exemplary, suddenly explode?' asked the press.†

* *Libération*, 8 October 1990.
† *L'Express*, 11 October 1990.

Little reference was made then, or is made now, to the link between the rage of the rioters and the behaviour of local police.

In 2005 Amnesty International delivered a stinging report on human rights abuses by the French police. The report claimed that police officers had been using 'excessive and sometimes lethal force against suspects of Arab and African origin without fear of serious repercussions'.* This situation, so similar to that which prevailed in Brixton and Toxteth in the early years of Thatcher's Britain, can only lead to rage and fury. And it does, at regular intervals. Each time a riot is started in one of France's ghettos, the mainstream French press, very largely echoed by the international press, looks around for the usual clichés. May '68 (that most bourgeois phenomenon) is invoked with monotonous regularity in order to avoid using the true term for what is really going on: a race riot.

Once again we're up against that blind spot in French consciousness: the Equality Myth. France does not have ethnic minorities. Instead, she has equal French citizens *in the process of integrating*. She does not, therefore, have ghettos, nor does she have race riots. The youths in these 'difficult suburbs' are angry because they are unemployed, or have no future, or are groping for an identity, or as François Mitterrand put it to his ministers in the aftermath of the Vaulx-en-Velin riots, living in places 'that provoke despair'.

* 'France: justice fails victims of police brutality', Amnesty International, 6 April 2005.

When, in the autumn of 2005, France's suburbs erupted in another series of riots, many English-language reporters, salivating over this diverting display of Gallic chaos, made an error of translation that subtly misrepresented reality. Nicolas Sarkozy – while on a visit to the housing estate in Clichy-sous-Bois where the riots began – was caught, on camera, in conversation with a woman in a high-rise block, who was leaning out of her window. Calling up to her, he gallantly promised to 'get rid of this *racaille* for you'. The Anglo-Saxon press translated *racaille* as 'scum'. The accurate translation for this rather archaic word would be *rabble*, not scum. Sarkozy would not have chosen the word scum – closer to *pourriture* or *salaud* in French. To do so would have been political suicide. Indeed, he chose the word *racaille* in part because it was the name that Arab youths called each other.

France's tradition of popular dissent, as much a part of her deepest nature as her desire to conform, makes the rest of the population very cautious about condemning any riots. After all, most social advances in French history were achieved through rebellion rather than reform. Social optimists see the suburban riots as proof that the sons and daughters of France's immigrants have, by virtue of their rage against the authorities, become truly French. Others react to the riots by revealing the equally powerful desire built into the French collective unconscious: the yearning for order and discipline. As de Gaulle once explained, 'France is not left-wing! France is not right-wing! The French naturally feel, as they always have, currents within them. There is the eternal current of motion that moves towards reform and change, which are necessary; and then there is the current of order, of rules and traditions, which are also necessary. All this is France.'

French people are divided – between each other and within themselves. When the rioters chant their hatred of the police, many French people find it hard to condemn them. As de Gaulle's minister Alain Peyrefitte put it, 'All French people, deep in their hearts, are in constant readiness to rise up against the State . . . the taste for rebellion, the nostalgia for revolution or at least revolt, the anarchist fantasy, the horror of order, of the "cop", the "pig", and of course its indivisible counterpart – the need for order, expeditious, merciless . . .'

The kind of liberal-humanist analysis that Mitterrand made about the suburbs provoking despair is no longer fashionable or credible. A new pseudo-scientific word has been invented to explain the nation's explosive suburbs: *La Conjoncture*. A favourite for the media, this is an untranslatable expression denoting (loosely) those aspects of the social and economic climate that cannot be changed, that are quite beyond the control of any politician and are, in many cases, the result of globalisation and, by extension, America.

France's War on Terror

No sooner had I deciphered the complex nature of French anti-Semitism than I began to realise that the staple diet of racism in France was in fact anti-Arab sentiment. Of all the Arabs migrating to France, the most unpopular are those that hail from the most enmeshed of her former colonies, Algeria. Anti-Algerian sentiment is not only rife, but also somehow permissible, blamed on either the thorny relationship existing between the two nations or on Algeria's bloody and bellicose nature. You will frequently hear people admitting to loving the Moroccans or the Tunisians but disliking the Algerians. Even Algerians themselves will be quick to mention any Kabyle (Berber) heritage they might have, rather than admit to being an Algerian Arab. France's relationship with Algeria makes Britain's relationship with India seem tranquil as a millpond by comparison.

In the early nineties, ten years before the rest of the Western world, France had become the main target of Islamist violence. As it turned out, the bombers were recruited and trained in Algeria. Just beneath the surface of the strange, theological language that was being used by this new generation of terrorists lay the old resentment of the colonised towards their oppressor. France was dragged early into this proto-war on terror because of her fraught and complex relationship with Algeria. Her continued involvement in the affairs of this nation, once a *département* of France, and her support for a deeply unpopular and corrupt regime that had been siphoning off the country's immense oil revenues for three decades, stirred up all the latent enmity left over from a particularly ugly war of independence.

In December 1991, during the Algerian general elections, a party known as the Islamic Salvation Front (FIS) seemed on the brink of victory. The party's fervent campaign among Algeria's poorest and its considerable achievements in bringing schooling and medical care to those rural and urban areas badly neglected by central government were about to pay off. On 27 December 1991, at the end of the first round, the FIS won 47 per cent of the vote. The results indicated that the party was likely, come the next round, to win two-thirds of the seats in the National Assembly. If this happened, the FIS could legally change the constitution and establish an Islamic state.

In January 1992, Algeria's highly unpopular president, Chadli Benjedid, declared the election results invalid, banned the FIS and dissolved the National Assembly. One week later, under pressure from the military, Chadli resigned and General Mohammed Boudiaf, hero of Algerian independence, took over as head of a governing council, thereby effecting a kind of soft coup that fooled no one. The FIS set about organising its military resistance and formed its armed wing, the Islamic Salvation Army (AIS). Concurrently, a rival armed group called the GIA was created. Its motto, 'No dialogue, no reconciliation, no ceasefire', was an augur of the increasing brutality of its methods.

Watching the unfolding chaos, President François Mitterrand decided to take the line of least resistance and do nothing. He neither condemned nor condoned the coup. He was, of course, uncomfortable about the interruption of the democratic process, but the prospect of an

Islamic state just across the Mediterranean was no more appealing, nor was the prospect of a massive influx of Algerian refugees.

Mitterrand's wait-and-see posture with regard to the civil war brewing in Algeria became increasingly untenable as the regime's campaign of repression escalated and the massacres of civilians, perpetrated by both sides, spread across the country. As the violence intensified, the Algerian regime called for more military and financial aid from its largest trading partner. France managed to hold back until early 1993, when she pledged 5 billion francs in aid and subsidies. By this time it had become clear that her vital interests and that of the Algerian regime were intertwined. Islamist guerrillas had begun targeting Algeria's francophone intellectuals and the nation's elite was fleeing for France.

Meanwhile, the French government came under ever-increasing pressure from Paris's intelligentsia to do something. Mitterrand was now in his twelfth year as president and sharing power with a centre-right government whose coercive policies were embodied in its hard-talking interior minister, the Corsican Charles Pasqua. On 4 November 1993, in response to pressure from French public opinion and the Algerian regime, Pasqua's police mounted a massive operation against individuals identified by the RG as Muslim fundamentalists or named by the Algerian secret services as FIS sympathisers. 'Operation Chrysanthemum' led to the arrest of eighty-eight people, many of whom were released through lack of proof and subsequently placed under surveillance or summarily deported to Burkina Faso. By the end of 1994, the French police had arrested almost two hundred people suspected of sympathy or involvement with the FIS.

So it was that France was drawn into Algeria's bitter civil war; a war that would last for ten years and leave an estimated two hundred thousand people dead and at least fifteen thousand missing. France's own body count in that war began on 21 September 1993, when the corpses of two French land surveyors were found with their throats cut in the hills close to Oran. In January 1994 a woman employed by the French consulate in Algiers was shot dead on the Place des Martyrs in broad daylight. After this, executions of French nationals escalated apace, culminating in the kidnapping of seven French Trappist monks who were taken from their monastery in the mountains south of Algiers in the early hours of the morning of 27 March 1996. Almost two months later, while France's two intelligence services (DST and DGSE) were busy tripping each other up in their respective negotiations to secure the release of the monks, a communiqué came from 'Emir' Djamel Zitouni, head of the Islamic Armed Group (GIA): 'We have cut the throats of the seven monks, as we promised. God be praised, it happened this morning.'

Nine days later the monks' heads were discovered near Médéa, each one resting on a white satin cloth with a rose beside it. The brutal nature of this crime, with its echo of Catholic martyrdom, caught France's attention. More than the massacre of entire villages, beheaded with chainsaws, the murder of the seven monks still stands, in France, as an emblem of the conflict.

By this time France was reeling from a wave of bomb attacks on her soil. The GIA's campaign had begun the summer before, on 5 July 1995, with an explosion in the Paris underground station of Saint-Michel, which had killed eight people. In the weeks that followed seven home-made bombs using gas canisters filled with nails were placed in stations, litter bins and market squares throughout the country. The Chirac government announced its 'Vigipirate Plan' and teams of armed troops began patrolling the streets and railway stations. It was a tense and frightening period. Paris, the city of ease and pleasure, could not get used to the sight of jackboots on the streets again. Military patrols stood guard outside Jack and Ella's school, and Laurent, who had always used the Metro, began cycling to work. People were all the more traumatised by the attacks when it emerged that the suspects were all Algerian, either born or raised in France.

At the end of August, a bomb was discovered on the high-speed TGV line between Paris and Lyon. It carried the fingerprints of Khaled Kelkal, a young man known to the police, not for religious extremism but for car theft. Kelkal, who was born in Algeria, grew up in Vaulx-en-Velin. An above-average student, enrolled in the baccalau-reate and with a particular gift for physics and chemistry, Kelkal was caught joy-riding and given a four-month prison sentence. When he returned to Vaulx he dropped out of school and took up armed robbery. In 1991 he was arrested and sentenced to four years in prison. Inside he found Islam.

Kelkal's profile confirmed France's worst fears of the terrorist nurtured in the bosom of the nation. And yet, as the manhunt for Kelkal got under way, it became clear that there was something reassuring about the cliché of this suburban youth gone awry and hijacked by religious extremists.

At the end of September 1995 the whole of France was riveted to the hunt for Khaled Kelkal. After months of fear, it seemed that a happy outcome was imminent. The new interior minister, Jean-Louis Debré, who had announced (rashly as it turned out) that he believed Kelkal to have been behind all the attacks, was having three meetings a day with the heads of all France's police forces. By the last days of September, the hunt for Kelkal had mobilised 760 men, including eight mobile units of the *Gendarmerie*, a platoon of parachutists, a SWAT team, sniffer dogs, as well as backup from the Territorial Army. Kelkal was tracked down to a bus stop called 'Maison Blanche', in the wooded hills 25 kilometres outside Lyon. The denouement, shown on France's main evening news, offered the poignant catharsis the nation so craved. Wounded in the leg, the twenty-four-year-old fugitive brandished his 1939 Mab pistol, which jammed, and under orders from the SWAT team leader, who yelled out for all to hear, '*Finis-le! Finis-le!*' (Finish him off!), the *Gendarmerie* opened fire.

The inevitable *mea culpa* that ensued was nipped in the bud by Prime Minister Alain Juppé, who firmly announced in the National Assembly the next day that he would not tolerate any suspicion: the *Gendarmerie* had fired in self-defence.

One month later a bomb exploded in the Paris Metro station Maison Blanche, in homage to the place where Kelkal had been shot. After Kelkal's death the bombing campaign continued until the end of the following year, culminating in an attack on Paris's Port-Royal RER station on 3 December 1996, which killed four people and wounded 170 others.

By this time the French government was under pressure to end its support for the regime in Algiers. French intellectuals had signed a petition for 'peace and democracy in Algeria', demanding that the French government stop 'all military assistance to the Algerian authorities'. Evidence was beginning to emerge that the Algerian regime had been waging a dirty war of horrendous proportions and that many of the brutal massacres of civilians, blamed on the Islamists, had been carried out by police and army death squads.* On 8 November 1997, in an interview with the *Observer*, a former employee of the Algerian secret service living in London revealed that Djamel Zitouni, the GIA's commander-in-chief who had ordered the assassination of the Monks of Tiberine and masterminded the Paris bombings, had been working for

* John Sweeney, 'Police role in Algerian killings exposed', *Observer*, 11 January 1998.

Algerian counter-terrorism.* Years later, Ali Touchent, whom French counter-terrorist police had identified as the man who had recruited Khaled Kelkal, was identified as an Algerian agent. Despite the extensive round-ups by French police and the subsequent dismantling of all Touchent's networks, both in France and Belgium, he miraculously eluded capture and returned to Algiers unmolested, where he settled under a police protection programme.

By this time, though, it was too late to change strategy. France had embarked on a policy of zero tolerance towards all forms of Islamic militancy, and the French public approved. By the end of the decade, as other Western nations got to know Islamic terrorism, France had become the envy of anti-terrorist forces the world over, boasting twelve years with no attacks on her soil. People in the field claim that France's success in combating terrorism is due to the close ties between the police and judiciary, specialised anti-terrorist courts and an impressive arsenal of detention and expulsion procedures. Success may also be due to a certain lack of vigilance when it comes to civil and human rights abuses and a loose consensus in the media that coercion in this domain is acceptable.

In keeping with her republican traditions, there is a widespread and accepted intolerance towards religion in France. This intolerance had always struck me as irrational, but

* Interview with Hocine Ouguenoune, former captain in the DCSA, Direction Centrale de la Sécurité de l'Armée (military intelligence).

after the bombing campaign of the nineties, it seemed to take on a new level of hysteria. In 2004, when Chirac's government banned the wearing of the *hidjab* (Islamic headscarf) in State schools, I was stunned by the ubiquitous support for a measure that I believed to be not only intolerant but counter-productive. I argued with all my French friends, and even my own children, who felt that there was no place for this religious symbol in the schools of the Republic. I was shocked by the vehemence with which I was attacked for supporting young girls who chose to wear the *hidjab*.

'You're condoning a symbol of male oppression,' my own daughter protested.

When I argued that banning this symbol would only radicalise a young woman likely to grow out of her religious fervour if left to her own devices, I was told that as an Anglo-Saxon, I would never understand. France had fought hard to disentangle herself from the stranglehold of religion. The separation of Church and State in 2005 was all too recent and France was as fervently attached to her secular identity (*laïcité*) as to any religion. Religious symbols were anathema to the Republic.

It has always been France's vocation to assimilate, my friends told me. British pragmatism – which accepts the idea of separate communities continuing to observe their own culture and traditions – is offensive to the French. It did not occur to any of them that France's Muslim communities *were* separated, not by their traditions, or their language, or their culture, but by economic and social exclusion and by their own alienation and rage.

Ten years later, in the aftermath of the 2005 July bomb attacks on London, I was shocked again, but this time by British commentators who were arguing that France's zero tolerance (in every sense of the word) had spared her from the horrors of terrorism. Later that same year, when France was reeling from another wave of suburban rioting in *les cités*, Britain could then return to her preferred position as back-seat driver and condemn France for the excesses of a zero-tolerance policy towards her immigrant communities.

Until Britain herself became a target, the approach of British intelligence, much to the irritation of the French, was always to observe Muslim extremism from a distance, intervening only if and when it posed a direct threat to national security. Jean-Louis Bruguière, one of France's leading anti-terrorist investigative magistrates, has been a fierce critic of this policy ever since he began his investigations into the Paris bombings of the nineties and discovered that the bombers were using London as their base. He became particularly irate when the British authorities refused to extradite Rachid Ramda, also known as Abou Farès, believed by Bruguière to have financed the Paris bombings of 1995.

'It's all very well, this blind-eye policy,' he told me at the time. 'You'll buy peace for a while. But believe me, your turn will come.'

When Britain's turn did come, the policy changed just

as Bruguière had predicted. Rachid Ramda's extradition was finally decided three months after the London bomb attacks. He was extradited in December of that year and on 26 October 2007, sentenced to life imprisonment by a French court.

Bruguière is the perfect symbol of France's answer to anti-terrorist policing. With his bodyguards, his blacked-out, armoured Peugeot, his .357 Magnum pistol – always peeking discreetly but clearly from his open jacket during our lunches together – Bruguière always brims with self-belief. This mega-star of the judiciary has dominated investigations into all the major threats to the French State over the past thirty years. From Carlos the Jackal (whom he had kidnapped by the French secret services in Khartoum) to Al Qaeda, this investigating magistrate has managed to place himself at the heart of French foreign policy and became, throughout the nineties, a kind of *éminence grise* to the Quai d'Orsay (France's foreign office). In October 1992 – while investigating Muammar Ghadafi's apparent involvement in the bombing of the UTA airline's DC-10 in September 1989, in which 170 passengers died on a flight from Brazzaville to Paris – Bruguière sailed to Tripoli on board a French Navy warship that had been lent to him by François Mitterrand. Libya, which was under a US-led blockade at the time, refused to let him in and he was turned back, but only after a magnificent photo opportunity featuring the magistrate standing on the deck of this massive frigate and looking like the scourge of Justice.

When I met Bruguière, the word on the street was that he would talk to anyone, provided they took him to a very good restaurant – preferably Robuchon's (named that year the best restaurant in the world by the *International Herald Tribune*). Although the BBC research budget did not stretch that far, he did accept lunch at Robuchon's former restaurant, Laurent. Once I had recovered from the excitement of dining with this swashbuckling hero of French counter-terrorism, it became clear that Judge Bruguière – once you looked behind the gun and the bodyguards and the aura of a man used to pacing the corridors of power – was, well, a little unstable. Distracted and excitable like many people of power, Bruguière's behaviour during our various meetings made me want to delve a little further into his world.

As in most Latin countries, France's judiciary follows the inquisitorial system. Heir to the infamous Catholic Inquisition, this system places a magistrate in charge of the police investigation. He or she leads the investigation, accumulating evidence both for the defence and the prosecution, right up until the hearing. When it comes to court, only the evidence presented by the investigating magistrate will be up for discussion. To some, this provides useful supervision to police work and thereby reduces the chances of police brutality during the investigation; to others, it merely slows things down and places too great a burden on a single – potentially corruptible – individual. Indeed, French judicial blunders tend to come not from police malpractice but from the fallibility of the investigating magistrate, who snaps under pressure. Bruguière, who comes from a long line of magistrates, stretching back through eleven generations, is immune to self-doubt. Known to his friends as 'The Admiral' since his escapade to Tripoli and as 'Sheriff' to his enemies (for his perceived sycophancy towards the FBI), Bruguière is said to love secrecy and conspiracy. He has, for many years, wanted Yves's former job as head of French counter-terrorism (DST), but has been passed over many times for less flamboyant men.

A firm believer in the policy of 'kicking the anthill', Bruguière's method, when it comes to Islamic terrorism, is to organise massive police operations resulting in large numbers of what he calls 'preventative arrests'.

'The goal is to keep constant heat on the Islamists,' he explained to me. 'By doing this you prevent networks from forming and deal with the problem before it happens.'

In July 1998 Bruguière mounted a police operation to dismantle suspected GIA sympathisers in France: 138 people were arrested in one day and Bruguière was broadly congratulated in the press for this deadly blow to terrorism. As it turned out, Bruguière's colleague Gilbert Thiel, who was forced to take over the investigation, dismissed thirty-four of the cases due to lack of evidence and released a further fifty-one people who had been sitting in prison for several months awaiting trial.

My lunches with Bruguière, though hugely diverting, did not provide me with any details of the cases he was investigating. I had to look elsewhere for those. An arch manipulator like the people in the intelligence world he so admired, Bruguière quite fittingly decided to have a run at political office. In March 2007 he rallied behind Nicolas Sarkozy's candidacy and ran for MP in the department of Lot-et-Garonne, where he tasted defeat, possibly for the first time in his life.

12 Sarkozy and the End of Ideology

Sex Dwarves and the Patriarchy

France's hapless former prime minister Dominique de Villepin once told an eminent journalist from *Le Figaro* that what France really needed was to be raped by a strong leader: '*La France veut qu'on la prenne*,' said the suave diplomat who is compared to Chateaubriand by his friends and the emperor Nero by his enemies: *France wants to be taken by force*.

Villepin's record for taking his nation's temperature is pretty poor. He was the man responsible for proposing and then withdrawing the labour reforms (CPE) of 2004 after six weeks of student mayhem and political deadlock. It seems, though, that on the matter of France's deepest desires, he was probably right.

In some ways, Nicolas Sarkozy's strategy – or at least posture – was to 'take France by force'. His presidential campaign was peppered with pugnacious, coercive vocabulary. He claimed to be answering what he called the nation's long-suppressed 'need for order, authority and firmness'. Distinguishing himself from the motherly, reassuring messages of his opponent, Ségolène Royal, he invited French citizens to vote for *la rupture*. When

France chose Sarkozy, she made a clear choice in favour of a certain violence to herself. What form that violence would take, no one seemed quite sure at the time.

For some, Nicolas Sarkozy would herald the breaking of the last levees against globalisation. For others, he would enable France at last to benefit from the buoyancy of the global economy. So far, and unsurprisingly given the economic context, he has done neither. One year on, his ratings were at an all-time low, with 72 per cent of the population dissatisfied with his performance. When asked about the reasons for their disapprobation, the majority of French people cited not his reform record but his *style* of governance, in particular his *médiatisation* or celebrity status. The French do not want a rock star as their head of State. It seems that they still prefer a kind of godhead (legacy of the divine right of kings) – aloof, disembodied and unaccountable.

It is interesting to note that in spite of the general dissatisfaction, France, a nation supposedly immune to change, has swallowed a large quantity of reforms. In his first year in office Sarkozy managed, with no major industrial action, to push through unprecedented legislation on France's traditionally immutable education system, as well as reforms to the labour code and the welfare system. But far more fundamental than all this is a deep and subtle mutation taking place in French society, simply by virtue of the fact that, in electing Nicolas Sarkozy, the population capitulated to a force that it had long resisted. More than its individual achievements and reforms, Sarkozy's presidency will be remembered as the turning point in French history, the moment when ideology began to die.

Since the 1789 Revolution, the dominant ideology – with the exception of the fascist interlude of Vichy – has been socialist. In French schools, Civic Education – an obligatory subject from the age of thirteen – teaches the values of the Republic and encourages youngsters to engage in political debate. The fact that both the creators of this discipline and its teachers were left-wing never seems to have posed a problem, for there has always been a broad consensus that socialist values and republican values were synonymous. The fact that there was a huge (silent) portion of the country that believed otherwise never appeared to bother the chattering classes, whose values and interests were consistently upheld by the media. This political reality explains why analysts were so stunned by the result of the referendum on the European constitution: no one predicted a 'No' vote because the press and television had so clearly supported a 'Yes' vote.

The remarkable thing about Nicolas Sarkozy is that he managed to get elected *without* the media. Sarkozy, who has long denounced the media's lack of objectivity, managed to ride out its powerful opposition to him and appeal directly to voters. Over the years he has gathered around him a heterogeneous array of supporters from right across the political spectrum and from all walks of life, thereby gaining a reputation as a freethinker. It was no doubt this image that appealed to many of his younger supporters (including my own son, Jack), who were bored by the ideological stranglehold of the post-'68 generation.

It has long been Sarkozy's wish to annex the moral high ground from the left, which has held it firmly ever since the Occupation. Indeed, Nicolas Sarkozy is the first French politician since Pétain to dare to invoke the values of order, work, merit and reward, claiming that these are the values of *common sense*, not of ideology. The recent political demise of Jean-Marie Le Pen (who lost many of his voters to Sarkozy) indicates that the president has had a measure of success in reclaiming the moral high ground for the right. With Le Pen, the left lost a very useful bogeyman, one which had long enabled them to stifle any serious debate.

Since becoming president, it has become clear that Sarkozy's offer of rupture was above all the offer of a break with ideology. For half the nation, the prospect of no longer having to take sides in endless and fruitless political debate is a welcome relief. For the other half, it means the end of life as they know it. All the reforms that Sarkozy managed to slip past the Assembly during the torpor of the first *Grandes Vacances* of his presidency threaten to put an end to the reign of ideology. But the most important of these reforms, the one that targets the beating heart of received ideas in France, is the reform of the university system.

Here, Sarkozy relied heavily on support from that element of French youth that is fed up with the legacy of May '68. Much has been written in recent years about the generation of bourgeois intellectuals, known as *les soixante-huitards* (sixty-eighters), who led the student uprisings against de Gaulle's stultified order. This is the generation that has fashioned the French political landscape, runs the mainstream media, has lived off the fat of the land and squandered a thriving economy in the process. Once the heroes of a glamorous revolution, the *soixante-huitard* is perceived, increasingly, as a selfish, hypocritical champagne socialist (*gauche caviar*).

For the hitherto silent majority that voted for him, Sarkozy is a self-made man who was not fashioned by the dominant ideology of his generation. On the wrong side of May '68, Sarkozy was never a member of the *gauche caviar* that lost its soul in the financial corruption scandals of Mitterrand's reign. Nor did he go to one of the *Grandes Ecoles*, those hot-houses of the French Republic that have, for centuries, churned out generations of politicians, both left and right, branding them with that special self-importance common to all members of France's elite. He is a truculent upstart and as such detested by a large portion of the bourgeoisie. At least, he must *appear* to be detested. For as one friend put it, 'The Sarkozy vote is a guilty vote [*vote honteuse*],' and the many millions of bourgeois who did vote for him do not admit to it.

To echo my son Jack's theory, the upstart Sarkozy is the conquering hero, the Nietzschean superman, whose extraordinary will to power, for a time, set him above the constraints of conventional French morality. This profile, for Jack, explains his election and his massive, though short-lived, popularity, as well as his ability, where all others have failed, to push through unwelcome reforms. It was Sarkozy's will to power combined with his conquering libido which, more than his policies, won the hearts, if momentarily, of the French people. His conquest of Carla Bruni, known as 'The Predator' for her voracious sexual appetite, only confirmed this popularity.

I would go one step further than Jack, however, and – borrowing from my sisters' rich vocabulary when it comes to the categorising of male sexual stereotypes – describe Nicolas Sarkozy as a *sex dwarf.* To my mind, what defines France's little president and explains his magnetism is not simply his 'will to power', but the particular circumstances that drive it: his small stature and his large sex drive.

In a culture unreconstructed by either of the great movements that have fashioned Anglo-Saxon society (Protestantism and feminism), the libido is still a force to be reckoned with, and the strange currents that brought Sarkozy to power would suggest that Dominique de Villepin was right: France did indeed wish to be taken by force.

It was widely observed that the last presidential elections were not a battle between left and right but rather a contest between two 'styles' – one gentle, the other tough; one consensual, the other coercive; one feminine, the other masculine. In the end, the French opted, not for the reassuring arms of Ségolène Royal and her 'gentle revolution', but for Nicolas Sarkozy, the libidinous sex dwarf, and his promise of 'rupture'.

All the iconography of the presidential campaign pointed to the subliminal forces that were dominating the battleground. Picture Ségolène Royal on the eve of the second round of the elections, dressed all in white, as if in homage to that alliance of virginity and female power embodied in such icons as Elizabeth I and Joan of Arc. Now picture Sarkozy, short and strutting in an oversized and sweat-stained suit, like France's favourite dictator, the potent and charismatic Napoleon Bonaparte.

Sarkozy, like Bonaparte, has all the characteristics of the sex dwarf: he is short, shamelessly flirtatious and tireless in his pursuit of women. Despite the fact that no record of his sexual conquests has ever been allowed to see the light of day, I don't need documentary evidence to prove that Sarko is a sex dwarf. I sensed it myself in 1996 when I was writing an article about French Protestants. As mayor of Neuilly he attended a fête being held by the Protestant community and somebody introduced us. I noticed as he shook my hand that he had the disquieting quirk common to many sex dwarves, which is that they look at your mouth when they're talking to you. His sexual magnetism has been broadly discussed, and his conquest of Cécilia, when, also as mayor of Neuilly, he officiated at her marriage to one of his closest friends, has become legend. It has been suggested that their affair began in that moment and that Cécilia's first husband 'had horns' even as they were exchanging their vows.

The next time I encountered Nicolas Sarkozy was in

2006 at a press conference that he gave as minister of the interior in order to trumpet the successes of the police forces under his command. I thought I had grown out of my tendency to blush, but throughout the event I thought, *Either I'm pre-menopausal or this person is going out of his way to embarrass me.* Hard as it is for me to admit, sitting in the tiny minister's line of vision for two hours was among the most erotically charged experiences I have had, and when he ended the conference and swept out of the room with his aides running behind him, I was left in a state of Victorian agitation. (If I had had a fan, I would have been waving it furiously.)

Afterwards, I asked a female colleague from French radio if she had noticed the minister's behaviour.

'Oh,' she said with a smile. 'He always does that. He finds a woman in the crowd and then undresses her with his eyes.'

My own feelings of attraction–repulsion during that press conference left me in no doubt: France's diminutive president is unquestionably a sex dwarf.

There is something baffling about Nicolas Sarkozy's meteoric rise to power, not only to the millions of people who didn't vote for him, but for many of the millions who did and who now, like my own children, regret it. His success can only really be explained in psychosocial terms. I suggest that it was the collective desire of the French people to be represented by a dominant and libidinous male, rather than a dominant and matriarchal female. This particular fantasy could only have found an outlet in a society unreconstructed by feminist ideology; in short, a Patriarchy. France, despite her many powerful women, is resolutely still a Patriarchy. The story of Ségolène Royal's political rise and fall is a perfect illustration of this.

When it became clear that a woman was emerging as the Socialist Party's candidate for the presidency, there was a ripple of excitement. Journalists, in particular, foresaw a more diverting contest than the uninspired locking of antlers they had come to expect; for many voters, either for or against her, the presence of a female candidate seemed to herald a new era in politics, a fresh start. It appears, however, that France was not quite ready for a female head of State.

Once the novelty had worn off, the matter of Royal's femininity began to undo her. Throughout, it was the leitmotif of her campaign, though not one of which she was always in control. Her gender was used as a weapon by both camps, either to aid or to hinder her rise to power. Her supporters brandished her feminine credentials, alternately championing the nurturing mother of four or the powerful and independent working woman, her opponents often attacking her for the same attributes. The most shocking assaults, however, came from her own camp. Jean-Luc Mélanchon, a colleague from the Socialist Party, on hearing of her triumph in the primaries said, 'The presidency of the Republic is not a beauty contest.'

And Laurent Fabius, her rival in the leadership contest, asked, 'Who will look after the children?'

As testimony to the confusion surrounding the issue of Royal's gender, *Libération* – which has always been resolutely anti-Sarkozy – referred to Royal, in as early as October 2005, as *La Maman de Fer* (the Iron Mother).

This kind of gender stereotyping would be unthinkable in Britain or America. In France it is routine. Too busy emancipating herself from her symbolic patriarch de Gaulle, France never actually took on the patriarchy itself.

When the time came in the Anglo-Saxon world for the roles men and women play to change, there was an unspoken agreement in France for them to stay the same. In the public sphere, things have advanced (France is only a little way behind Britain when it comes to the number of women in parliament), but in private, nothing much has moved. Men still feel they can accost women in the street to compliment them on their beauty and, as my own daughter has shown me, most women wait for the man to make the first move. Few people, even those who have fought for women's rights, refer to themselves as feminists, and the word sexist as a term of abuse is rarely used.

Women in patriarchies are tough on each other. A measure of this lies in the fact that the most misogynistic comments came from Ségolène Royal's own gender. Michèle Alliot-Marie, the Chirac government's defence minister, said of Royal's performance in a televised debate with Sarkozy: 'Being vague is fine for fashion, not for politics.'

Another left-leaning publication, the news magazine *Le Nouvel Observateur*, conducted a survey in which one hundred famous women were questioned on their feelings about the socialist candidate. The majority of them disliked her – their principal objection having something to do with her being the mother of four. Their grievance was summed up by a comment made by the former porn star Brigitte Lahaie: 'For her [Royal], the image of the mother overrides the image of the woman.'

Or as Virginie Despentes, controversial author of the novel *Baise-Moi* (*Fuck Me*), said, 'When Royal calls for the army in the suburbs, it is not the virile figure of the law . . . but the extension of the absolute power of the mother.'

It is both odd and telling that porn star and feminist alike express this culture's entrenched mistrust of the overbearing mother. In the end, the women of France were Royal's harshest judges, expressing an eloquent and varied misogyny and relaying the deepest fears of the male psyche. Catherine Millet, author of *The Sex Life of Catherine M*, said of her: 'She's a Robespierrette. This country doesn't need a "Mummy" to give it moral lectures.'

As a national poll revealed, in the first round of the elections even Royal's own voters were in some doubt as to her suitability for supreme office, only 16 per cent of them believing that she had the 'stature' of a president. As is often the case with this extremely idealistic and at the same time conservative nation, the *idea* – in this instance, of a woman as president – was considerably more appealing than the reality.

Throughout her campaign, Royal herself vacillated on

the matter of whether or not to exploit her femininity, sometimes castigating people for alluding to her gender and sometimes brandishing it as her main argument: 'I know that certain electors, male and female, ask themselves if it isn't too revolutionary to vote for a woman. Well I say to them: be that audacious because France will feel a wonderful breath of innovation and you won't regret it.'*

Royal sometimes even fell prey to the very stereotyping she denounced by identifying her values as essentially feminine: 'The time for women has come so that the House of France can be rebuilt on good foundations: the family, education, employment, ecology . . .'

France has a long way to go when it comes to challenging sexual stereotypes. It was telling that TV journalists commenting on the debate between the two finalists repeatedly called the socialist candidate 'Ségolène' but never once used Sarkozy's Christian name. A cartoon in the left-wing satirical magazine *Charlie Hebdo* pictured Royal as a housewife, rifling through a bargain bin marked 'SALE' with the caption, 'The socialist programme at −50%. It's unbelievable!'

Royal's relationship with her domineering father has often been cited as the motor for her career, just as Sarkozy's philandering and absent father has been seen as the driving force behind his will to power. Unlike Sarkozy, however, Royal has had to struggle, not only against a single patriarch, but against the entire patriarchy. When she

* TF1, 26 April 2007.

appeared on the balcony of the Socialist Party headquarters on the night of her defeat, the radiance of her smile spoke of the relief of the natural runner-up. It was as if she had never really envisioned herself as the victor, as if on some subliminal level she had ingested the rules of the patriarchy and not *allowed* herself to imagine her own victory. Her face did not express disappointment, even as she mouthed the words: 'From the bottom of my heart I thank the 13 to 17 million voters who had confidence in me and I take the measure of their disappointment and their pain.'

It was *their* disappointment and pain, not hers, for as the air filled with the poignant, enraptured cry of her supporters – '*Merci Ségolène! Merci Ségolène!* – the face of this defeated woman expressed pure joy.

The Society of the Spectacle and the End of the Secret Garden

What most people seem to regret about the rise to power of Nicolas Sarkozy are the changes he has brought, not so much to the machinery of French society, but to its ethos. The most profound of these is the slow but steady invasion of celebrity culture and with it the very Anglo-Saxon fascination for the lives of other people: our Protestant taste for transparency and the concomitant tendency towards the witch-hunt; our snooping tabloids; our intrusive, fly-on-the-wall documentaries; our fixation with the sex lives of our politicians, celebrities and even next-door neighbours – all seem finally to be taking root in France.

Even Sarkozy's decision to divorce his wife was a signal of a profound mutation. In the past, the D word was simply not an option for a French president. In the French Catholic spirit of compromise, all presidents since the war – with the exception of the dour de Gaulle – were known, even expected to be unfaithful, and their wives either suffered in silence, or, as in the case of Danielle Mitterrand, cultivated their own *jardin secret*. But French opinion on the extramarital shenanigans of Nicolas and Cécilia Sarkozy has undergone a subtle shift. The public processing of misdemeanours, common to Protestant cultures, and the taste for smut that comes with it are seeping into French society.

In recent years, French celebrity magazines, modelling themselves on publications like *Hello!* and *OK!*, have dramatically increased their sales. *Closer* (pronounced 'Closœur'), introduced to this country in 2005 by the British magazine publisher Emap, is now the most popular magazine in France. In a single year, between July 2006 and July 2007, *Closer* saw its circulation rise by 55 per cent. This was due, in large part, to the magazine's decision to print photographs of the presidential candidate Ségolène Royal in her bikini while on holiday with her family, an intrusion that would never have happened in the more austere days of the Fifth Republic. The photos caused outrage among the chattering classes, who protested that French politics was becoming contaminated by Anglo-Saxon prurience.

Celebrity culture has been slow to arrive, but it appears

to be here. For many, President Sarkozy is to blame for breaking the taboo that had kept it at bay for so long. With his Rolex, his reflective Ray-Bans, his Dior suits, his glamorous, peripatetic ex and his supermodel/pop star wife, France's president is sending out a powerful and radical message: *It is OK to live the high life.* In other words, France seems to have reached that pivotal moment in the evolution of capitalist societies when, as Guy Debord put it in his book *La Société du Spectacle*, 'the commodity completes its colonisation of life'.

France's old guard – paradoxically embodied now in the May '68 generation – despises Sarkozy and his family for what it calls the Hollywoodisation of the French presidency. Cécilia and Nicolas chose to live their lives in the public eye, inviting *Paris Match* into the Elysée and putting their children on display. Sarkozy's very public mediation of his marital difficulties were a far cry from the discretion of Mitterrand – who for years managed to shame the French press into silence not only over his numerous infidelities but also his 'secret family' with Anne Pingeot.

Unlike the private Mitterrand, the fifty-four-year-old Sarkozy is a perfect product of Debord's 'society of the spectacle' – a symptom of end-stage capitalism in which 'the social relation between people is mediated by images'.

For the first time, France has a president who appears to have no complex about using the press to bolster his image. As did the young prime minister Tony Blair, all those years ago, he is exercising a new skill: the manipulation of the media in the fabrication of his persona. He does so in a way that seems archaic and blunt to a British audience. An example of his tactical subtlety was his request that one of his aides roll his son Louis's ball into the room during an interview so that the little boy could run in after it and have his father playfully throw it back to him. He wished, at the moment when his marriage was on the rocks, to maintain the illusion of a devoted father and committed family man. Unfortunately, Sarkozy's attempt to become France's answer to JFK backfired. He made the mistake of repeating the trick, and word got out.

There is strong resistance from the Parisian bourgeoisie to the subtle moral shift manifested in this new presidential style. An editorial in *Libération*, commenting on his glitzy life with Cécilia, expressed alarm at the president's capacity for marrying 'the two worlds of Politics and the Society of the Spectacle'. The journalist went on to lament the couple's lack of what the French call *pudeur*, a word that expresses the dual notion of shame and modesty: 'They descend from their private jets and walk the corridors of power as a family, visibly preyed upon by their personal crises, their childhood neuroses, their staged obsessions.'

Just beneath this criticism of the Sarkozys' histrionics lay an underlying disgust at the display of wealth. Indeed, as our own recent history has taught us, the first stage in the elaboration of a full-blown celebrity culture is the destruction of any taboos associated with the accumulation of money. France, through the person of her president, is taking the first steps towards complete equanimity about being 'filthy rich'. It seems that in order for celebrity culture to flourish, there must first be broad acceptance that the accumulation of wealth is a worthy goal.

In France's culturally Catholic society, this has never before been the case. Hence the outrage from a small section of France's elite when Sarkozy chose to spend his much-publicised post-election 'retreat' on the yacht of one of his billionaire friends. For millions of other French men and women, however, the sight of their new president sunning himself off the coast of Malta was a welcome change from the dour austerity of his predecessors. Indeed, it is a measure of how far public opinion has evolved since his election that the cries of outrage from the mainstream press have died to a whisper. Few of the newspaper editors of the '68 generation now bother to take on the subject of Nicolas and Carla's exhibitionism. Although today 72 per cent of the population claim to be dissatisfied with their 'bling bling' president, it is – as our own history has shown us – only a matter of time before the elitist levees break. Once the accumulation of wealth ceases to be taboo, it is a small step to an all-out, aspirational capitalism with its cohorts – competitive materialism and celebrity culture.* As Guy Debord would put it, the French, who have declined from 'being' to 'having', will now decline further 'from having into merely *appearing*'.

* Oliver James, *Guardian*, 3 January 2008.

13 Black, Blanc, Beur

Football, Rap and Role Models

In the summer of 1998 I took my thirteen-year-old son, Jack, on a road trip to Marseille to see the quarter-final of the World Cup. Laurent was probably grateful for a short break from our troubled and troublesome boy. All their conversations in those days – invariably on the subject of Jack's marks and behaviour at school – seemed to end in recrimination and despair. It was a hard time in Jack's life. He was about to be expelled from his sixth school and the only thing he cared about in the world was football.

We drove out of Paris on the morning of 1 July. Our plan was to stop off for the night with Laurent's uncle and aunt in their house in Puyméras, the village in Vaucluse where we had spent our honeymoon. There, Jack and I would watch the England–Argentina match together and see David Beckham sent off in the second half for kicking out at Diego Simeone. Jack, whose heart was perfectly divided between his love of the English and French squads, was fighting tears. He worshipped, in equal measure, two of the most dissimilar sportsmen you could find, Alan Shearer and Zinédine Zidane.

I had mixed feelings about our journey. On the one

hand, I was fearful of finding myself in a one-to-one with my son, whose debilitating anger could either make him sleep all hours of the day or else explode at the slightest provocation. On the other, I was grateful for the chance to be with this boy who could make me laugh like no one else and who had the most original take on the world of anyone I had ever met.

We both knew that we would not find much solace in French radio, with its obligatory quota of French pop music. Since 1994, in its inimitable style the State, pushed by the CSA (*Conseil Supérieur de l'Audiovisuel*, the French equivalent of Ofcom), had passed a law* stating that 40 per cent of any radio's playlist must be music written in the French language. Because of this, both Jack and I were grateful for French rap, which had been flourishing since the early nineties and brought a welcome change from the Eurovision-style mediocrity of French crooners and breathy actresses. I, like most parents, favoured the 'soft' rap of artists like MC Solaar, whose rich lyricism and elaborate wordplay turned my son, at least while he was reciting the songs, into a poet.

To put us in the mood, Jack put on an album called *L'Ecole du Micro d'Argent* by a rap group from Marseille called IAM. It had been released the year before to huge, even international, acclaim, and Jack knew every song by heart. Unlike Solaar, an existentialist who confines himself to the minutiae of his own experience, IAM's rapper,

* The Pelchat amendment (article no. 9488), 1 February 1994.

Akhenaton, with his distinctive lisp and suppressed rage, found words for the collective anger of kids raised in France's suburbs.

While I drove, I would cast discreet glances at my boy, sitting beside me mouthing the words of these angry, disinherited young men. His favourite number, 'Petit Frère', tells of the pattern of emulation operating in the ghettos and how the little brothers of the gangsters get caught up in the violence and crime.

> *Petit frère a déserté les terrains de jeux,*
> *Il marche à peine et veut des bottes de sept lieues,*
> *Petit frère veut grandir trop vite,*
> *Mais il a oublié que rien ne sert de courir, petit frère . . .**

The words seemed addressed directly to Jack. At the time he had found his own graffiti tag and was going into the tunnels of the Metro after school to make his mark. He had started smoking and, unbeknownst to me, was going into the suburbs of Saint-Denis to score hash. Soon I would be getting heart-stopping calls at 2am from the local *commissariat*:

'Madame Lemoine? [That officious, warning voice.] We have your son Jack in police custody [*garde à vue*] . . .'

On one occasion the *commissaire* had threatened to press charges for possession of cannabis. In desperation I

---

* 'Little brother has deserted the sports fields, / He can hardly walk and he wants seven-league boots, / Little brother wants to grow up too fast, / But he has forgotten that there's no point running, little brother . . .'

rang my friend from the *Renseignements Généraux*, who gave his colleague a call. The man offered a compromise. He would keep Jack in a police cell for six hours 'to give him a fright' and then I could come and pick him up. When I went to fetch him, they brought him to me in handcuffs. The French police, encouraged by successive governments and backed by the majority of the electorate, have a draconian attitude towards cannabis. When I saw my son so shamed, in cuffs, his head hanging, I was furious. Knowing, however, that they could keep him for another six hours on a whim, I stayed silent, signed for him and led him out into the sunshine.

Like all his friends at the time, Jack had seen Mathieu Kassovitz's *La Haine* (*Hate*), a beautiful tragedy, shot in black and white, about the day in the life of three friends living in one of Paris's suburbs. It had come out in 1995, when he was ten and he and his friends had, for the first time, seen how the other half lived. Ever since *La Haine* – which focused on the hair-trigger relationship between suburban youths and the police – Jack's role models were not the big brothers of his bourgeois peers from central Paris, but Arab youths (*beurs*) from the *cités*. He spoke like them with his hands, using quaint, chivalric expressions like *ma parole* (on my honour) and an elaborate language called *verlan* borrowed from the suburbs and originally designed to faze the authorities. French and Arabic and even *patois* words are turned inside out and back to front. (*Verlan* is the word *l'envers* – 'backwards' – pronounced backwards.) *Le flic* (cop) becomes *le keuf. Femme* (woman) becomes *meuf*. *Ma mère* (my mother) becomes *ma reum*. The word *beur*, used for and by the children of France's North African immigrants, comes from the *verlan* word *rebeu*, meaning 'Arab'. Jack could be on the phone talking to his friends and I would not understand a single word of what he was saying.

Le verlan is in constant flux, and Jack no longer speaks the contemporary version. Like so many things in this monolithic culture, there is the *idea* (the legendary rigidity of *l'Académie Française*) and then there is the *reality*. Despite the best efforts of the Republic to fix and codify the language, this vibrant, ever-changing patois of the streets eludes all classification and regulation. Like the *banlieue* that engendered it, *le verlan* is cut off from mainstream culture, a symbol of exclusion and banishment, and is used as a kind of talisman against compliance by millions of alienated teenagers.

Like the Arab males he was emulating, Jack would greet a friend with the beautiful gesture of ghetto Muslims, placing his hand on his heart and sweeping their palm. He would dress in tracksuits, favouring the brands Sergio Tacchini, Le Coq Sportif, or better still, Lacoste – at the time virtually the symbol of Arab youth.

Nothing could have been better calculated to irritate these children's bourgeois, *soixante-huitard* parents than speaking and dressing like an Arab youth. It drove Jack's father mad.

Marseille is a city that most Parisians can't stand. It is seen as dirty, lawless and full of Arabs. The first port of call for many immigrants from the Maghreb, it is both in atmosphere and outlook more like Algiers or Tunis than any French port. Marseille is rebellious, wild and cocky. It is also the only place in France, with the exception of Corsica, that still has a thriving local mafia, *Le Milieu*, which shares its huge revenue from slot machines, gaming and prostitution between a handful of families.

Marseille, France's oldest city, was founded by Greek Phocaeans around 600 BC and destroyed by Julius Caesar roughly half a millennium later. Louis XIV, fed up with its defiant independence, built a citadel to supervise its inhabitants and then sent in the army. The Nazis hated it, calling it 'a breeding ground for the mongrelisation of the Western world'. Today, despite the millions that have been poured into the rehabilitation of France's second-largest city, Marseille is still the bête noire of the French bourgeoisie. In terms of sheer antipathy her football team, *l'Olympique de Marseille* (OM), is to Paris's team, *Paris Saint-Germain* (PSG), what Manchester United is to Liverpool.

I have never understood the Parisian scorn for Marseille. The first time I went there I was dazzled; by the blanched light and deep-blue skies, washed clean by the Mistral, the golden stone of the buildings, the gentle rise of the city above the Vieux Port (Old Port), bold and busy and open-armed to the Mediterranean. I loved the bustle and the noise and the fact that every night the magnificent, rectangular port becomes a racetrack for errant youths and a detrital paradise for stray dogs. And every morning at 7am, the fishing boats arrive and the men and women of *la criée* (fish market) set up their stalls along the Quai des Belges, dripping with the night's plunder: squid and turbot, sea urchins and sardines.

We were going to Marseille, Zidane's home town and in many ways the capital of French football. Unlike so many French clubs, Marseille's sixty-thousand-seat stadium, Le Vélodrome, was regularly sold out, and its supporters could equal any British club for enthusiasm, though certainly not for the creativity of its anthems. Both Jack and I were drawn to Marseille for different reasons: Jack because it was by far the coolest city in France at the time, and I because I had had my fill of the Parisian bourgeoisie and needed an antidote.

Marseille, or *Planète Mars* as the local rap scene calls it, inspires awe and envy in the hearts of rival ghettos. The kids on *Planète Mars* can swim in the sea or go riding in the wild marshlands of the neighbouring Camargue or go fishing for sea bream off the rocks near the Prado, Marseille's largest beach. They seem less jaded than their brothers in Paris or Lyon, less enraged by what French society has to offer them.

Zinédine Zidane, whose parents are Kabyles from the mountains of Algeria, was brought up in the tower blocks of La Castellane, one of Marseille's northern ghettos. Already perceived as France's first great symbol of Arab integration, Zizou became a national hero that summer. He was part of a new generation of footballers, many of them born in France's immigrant ghettos, who would convince France – for a while at least – that she was a truly multicultural society. As the team went from win to win, it began to catch the nation's attention. Banners appeared on the terraces bearing the slogan *Black Blanc Beur*, a triumphant, multi-racial version of the French *tricolore*. Le Pen began ranting about the so-called 'non-representativity' of the French football team and berating goalie Fabien Barthez for not singing 'La Marseillaise'. But even he could not spoil the party. The leader of the *Front National* was gagged, at least for a while, when the whole nation, particularly French housewives, who had started to watch football for the first time, fell head over heels in love with the team. Bourgeois Parisian women started arguing over lunch about who was sexier – Zinédine Zidane or Youri Djorkaeff.

The fervour and enthusiasm that the French squad inspired that summer seemed greater than ever before. The phenomenon was subsequently labelled and analysed in a typically French way as 'The World Cup Effect'; namely, the momentary sweeping away of all prejudice and intolerance by the purifying power of desire.

The day after the team qualified for the final, the architect and left-wing thinker Roland Castro announced, 'Le Pen has gone quiet . . . We are witnessing in France the first retreat of the extreme right.'*

As it turned out, four years later the National Front had clawed back almost 20 per cent of the national vote

---

* *Libération*, 10 July 1998.

and Le Pen was the only candidate running against Chirac in the second round of the presidential elections. In October 2001, in the aftermath of 9/11, a friendly match between France and Algeria had ended in rioting and animosity. Algerian supporters had chanted support for Bin Laden and yelled out 'Traitor!' at Zidane. Twenty minutes before the end of the game, fans invaded the pitch. Zidane, who had helped engineer this historic game, had called it 'the worst moment of my career'.

Back then, however, in the summer of 1998, Jack and I, along with the rest of France, believed that Le Pen and his party were dead and this was the dawning of a new era for France.

When we arrived at the Old Port we took the road along the *corniche* to explore the coastline. We had been driving for about five minutes when we came round a corner. Jack yelled out, 'Mum! Look!' I braked. There, towering above us, covering the whole of the side of an apartment building and gazing out across the sea to the Old Port, was the face of Zinédine Zidane. The expression on his handsome face was stern and serene at the same time. 'This city belongs to people like me now,' it seemed to say, 'so get used to it.' When the World Cup ended and Adidas, who had sponsored the fresco, was asked to remove it, the whole city came out in protest. Ten years later, Zizou is still there, lording it over the Vieux Port. Now, though, in this unyielding and polarised age of *tolérance zéro*, his soft-hard face seems to express sadness and regret.

*

Despite a white paper made public in 2004, which described the situation in France's suburbs as 'more than preoccupying', little has changed for the children of France's African and Arab immigrants. The Ministry for Towns still suffers from the excessive bureaucracy and financial waste denounced by the report. Nineteen ministers for towns in fourteen years, all of them as eager to change jobs as was the case with the Northern Ireland secretary in British politics.

Determined to break the pattern when he came to power, Nicolas Sarkozy chose a woman of Kabyle origin who had herself been brought up in the tower blocks of Clermont-Ferrand. Fadela Amara, Sarkozy's minister for towns, is a fighter. At fourteen she saw her five-year-old brother Malik being run over by a drunk driver. The police who came to the scene of the crime defended the driver. Fadela lashed out at one of them, who then bombarded her with racist insults. Her little brother died from his injuries and her *cité* went up in flames.

Fadela is used to getting results. She began her political career at the age of sixteen when the mayor threatened to bulldoze her *cité*. She set about organising a petition and it was rehabilitated instead. In 2003 – to protest against a spate of gang rapes of young girls in the suburbs and the horrific death of Sohane Benziane, a seventeen-year-old girl who was burnt alive by a former boyfriend for rejecting him – Amara set up the association *Ni Putes Ni Soumises* (Neither Whores Nor Victims) and organised a huge march on the centre of Paris. The march, Amara said, was 'to say no to the constant and unacceptable degradation to which the girls in our suburbs are subjected and to utter a cry of rage'.

There must have been times when Sarkozy has regretted calling in Amara. When he put his old friend the draconian Brice Hortefeux at the head of the newly named, catch-all Ministry of Immigration, Integration, National Identity and Development in Solidarity (*Ministère de l'Immigration, de l'Intégration, de l'Identité Nationale et du Développement Solidaire*), there were bound to be sparks. Sure enough, Amara rejected Hortefeux's proposed legislation to carry out DNA testing on the children of immigrants to determine their parentage, calling it 'disgusting'.

When Amara arrived in her new office, she protested about the impenetrable bureaucracy of her ministry. 'You need a doctorate to understand what's going on,' she said. 'We need to simplify, democratise all this.'

In June 2008, after a long wait, Amara unveiled President Sarkozy's plan for the suburbs to the French public.

'I'm a pain in the arse,' she announced at the press conference. 'I got what I wanted.'

The scheme carries the suitably idealistic title, 'Hope Banlieue'. It represents a total investment of a billion and a half euros over three years and will focus on the two, uncontroversial, areas most in need of attention: employment and policing.

It will be a long haul for Amara and, tenacious as she has proven herself to be, she is fighting against a huge resistance to change. The French middle classes and the media that represents them do not want a multicultural society. They want the Republic to remain as it is, with its ideals and myths intact. They do not want to see Arab women in headscarves outside the gates of the Ecole de la République. They do not want positive discrimination, or affirmative action. They want francophone Africans to speak beautiful French, like MC Solaar, and play beautiful football, like Lilian Thuram.

Sarkozy could never have chosen Fadela Amara as a minister unless she had come out against the *hidjab*. Her feminist convictions guaranteed that she would. Indeed, when in 2008 the *Conseil d'Etat* (Supreme Court) refused French nationality to a Moroccan woman on the grounds that she wore a burka, Amara applauded the decision. For a woman, she said, 'the burka is a prison, a straightjacket . . . There is no difference between the headscarf and the burka.'*

There are no statistics on France's ethnic communities because ethnic or community-based data analysis is simply illegal. As a result, it is difficult to make real changes to the lives of the children and grandchildren of France's immigrants because the equality fable makes it taboo even to study them.

The language of that 570-page white paper on the suburbs probably reveals more about France than the content itself. It is so amazingly rarefied and out of touch: 'The

* *Le Figaro*, 16 July 2008.

situation of a large proportion of these populations, born of the most recent wave of immigration . . . apart from being frequently belittling, is the direct or indirect cause of serious social or racial tensions, heavy with danger for the future.'*

Thirteen years after *La Haine*, whose clever dialogue and self-conscious aestheticism got the French middle classes to pay attention to the matter of *la banlieue* for the first time, France is still hurtling towards impact.

'It's the story of a society in freefall,' the film concludes. 'In order to reassure itself, it repeats endlessly, "so far so good, so far so good" . . .'

* Report by the Cour des Comptes, 7 November 2004.

14 Epilogue

Douce France

For ten years, ten years too many, I was close to this milieu that refers to itself as 'All Paris' and which endlessly repeats the same things in the same tone without ever getting tired of its own ennui and convinced that it is exerting an influence upon society when it is no longer exerting any influence, even on fashion.

François Mitterrand, *L'Abeille et l'Architecte*

I would eventually discover that there was another side to France than the brittle, highfalutin, self-important world of the Parisian bourgeoisie. France's rural identity, despite the entrenched centralism of Paris's ruling elite, is alive and kicking. Indeed, one of the striking things about France's dual nature (urban and rural) is the extent to which one exists in perfect isolation from and ignorance of the other. The affairs of State grind on while France's peasant population – proud of this title and the knowledge and traditions that come with it – make their wine, tend their flocks or plough their fields with the same disregard for Parisian politicking that their fathers and forefathers showed before them.

I now live deep in the Cévennes Mountains of southern France, one of the nation's few Huguenot strongholds.

Epilogue

This is the place where, in 1878, Robert Louis Stevenson went for a very long walk with a donkey. Before that it was the place where French Protestants had been persecuted almost consistently by the French Catholic monarchy for over 120 years. It is a place of hardship and mind-boggling resilience: the very opposite of Gide's 'softness, surrender [and] relaxation in grace and ease'. The great nineteenth-century French historian Jules Michelet said of this place: 'The Cévennes offer rock, nothing but rock, razor-sharp shale. You feel the struggle of man, his stubborn and prodigious labour in the face of nature.' This place is a French aberration: a Protestant stronghold in the heart of a Catholic country.

The *Cevenols*, the descendants of those men and women who chose the Protestant Reformation five centuries ago, are inhabited by different values and traditions to their neighbours in the Catholic plains of the Languedoc. They champion integrity, punctuality, rigour and hard work over beauty, charm, art and leisure. They have a history of tolerance towards all minorities and distinguished themselves during the war by overwhelmingly choosing the Resistance and offering asylum to Jews on their flight to Spain.

It is a sweltering afternoon in June with not a breath of wind. It's too hot for birdsong, only the drone of insects and the sound of my neighbours working outside my window, gathering the hay. Three generations out in the midday sun, raking the pasture: grandfather, mother and grandson. They can't get the tractor up onto the steeply terraced land. Last week, the old man had spent a morning out there with a scythe, his hunched back moving slowly and methodically over the long grass, his arms making an even, sweeping motion. 'There's an old quince tree blocking the only access wide enough for the tractor. It's on its last legs,' he says with a smile. 'Sometimes one finds oneself wishing it would die,' he adds, taking off his beret and wiping the sweat from his brow. They wouldn't cut down the tree, of course. For one thing, it provides fruit. So they go round it. And mow the whole meadow, about 2 acres, by hand.

Many of my neighbours have never been to Paris and have no desire to go there. Those who have often did so under duress, to pick up a medal for Resistance activity during the Occupation or to attend the annual *Salon de l'Agriculture* (Agriculture Forum), now a media fest in which reluctant Parisian politicians, posing with prize cows and *saucisson*, scramble for the farmer's vote.

Little has changed since President Georges Pompidou remarked to Alain Peyrefitte in 1969 that 'France remains an old agricultural nation and agriculture has lost its value in the modern world . . . the new society, the new social contract, change – that's a language for Parisian intellectuals who can't tell a cow from a bull'.

I do not read *Libération* any more. Or *Le Monde*. They're impossible to get in my local village. Instead I'll pick up the occasional copy of *Midi Libre*, the regional newspaper founded, of course, by one of the Resistance movements in 1944. In today's copy is an article entitled

'*La lutte des classes n'a pas cessé d'exister*' (The class struggle
still exists). It's a quote from an interview with a local
trade unionist called Jacques who joined the miners'
union in 1944. The subtext of the article is an entrenched
and bitter hatred of capitalism and a powerful resistance
to Sarkozy's reforms.

'With the present government,' Jacques says, 'which is
hacking away at all our workers' rights and with Europe
trying to establish itself without the people, we are storing
up our rage. But class-consciousness is coming back and
the struggle has always existed. I'm optimistic. One day,
the people will win.'

This enduring and entrenched anti-capitalism of the
provinces, far more than the eyebrow-raising of the
Parisian elite, is the force most likely to thwart President
Sarkozy. No matter how fast and furious his programme
of reform (contrary to what has been reported by the
British press, the Sarkozy government managed to push
through more than sixty reforms in its first year), the president is unlikely to be able to change this country in one
mandate. He has been clever, though, particularly in his
reform of what is known as *le code du travail* (labour
code). The job market has, in France, been resolutely
immune to all attempts at liberalisation. Unlike his predecessors, President Sarkozy has avoided taking the unions
head-on. Instead, he cleverly rolled back the arbitrating
power of the State by allowing management and its
employees a greater freedom to negotiate with each other
directly.

Traditionally, one of the oddities of French trade unions was that a movement derived its right to negotiate on behalf of a company's employees, not from its *representativity* (number of members), but from its so-called *legitimacy*, adjudicated by the State, usually on the basis of a perceived historical legitimacy. One of the five criteria taken into consideration by the State in determining the 'legitimacy' of a union was the said union's behaviour during the Second World War: 'the patriotic attitude during the Occupation'. This made for a particularly rigid environment for labour relations, in which it was virtually impossible for any new movement to gain any traction. By encouraging direct negotiations, Sarkozy has subtly but radically changed the landscape. From now on only representative unions, i.e. those whose members make up at least 30 per cent of a company (and in the years to come that will increase to at least 50 per cent), are allowed to negotiate labour reforms. These negotiations, conducted under the new rules, will include a vote on the thirty-five-hour week. So Sarkozy will manage to dismantle this hugely divisive principle without even having to change the law. France's largest union, the *Confédération Française Démocratique du Travail* (CFDT) – which fought hard for the thirty-five-hour week – is of course furious. The mass demonstrations they organised in the spring of 2008 were a flop, however. People, it seemed, were tired of marching. And they wanted more money, not more leisure.

Things are changing, quietly, behind the scenes of government, while only a few irate militants howl their rage into the wilderness. There is the dismantling of the *régimes spéciaux*, a vestige of the old system of feudal privileges, by which the French monarchy and then the State granted 'special' retirement schemes to certain sectors deemed to be of particular service to the nation, as well as those occupations perceived by the State as particularly gruelling (*pénible*) – like driving a lorry, or a train, or working down a mine, or being a policeman or a soldier. Beneficiaries of this 'special' regimen also include sailors (since 1673), fishermen (since 1709), employees of the Bank of France (since 1806), actors with the *Comédie Française* (since 1812) and employees of the Paris Opera (since 1698), to whom Louis XIV kindly granted retirement and a pension from age forty for the dancers and fifty for the singers. For decades successive governments had tried to dismantle this absurd system of privileges, enjoyed by a mere 5 per cent of the population, but the determination of those concerned to hold on to their historic rights was so powerful and so impressive that it seemed to persuade the other 95 per cent of the justice of their cause. As Charles de Gaulle said, 'Every Frenchman wants to enjoy one or several privileges; it's his way of showing his passion for equality.'

In the end it was Nicolas Sarkozy, with his rather Anglo-Saxon love of common sense and plain speaking, who managed to break the taboo and get public opinion behind the principle of equity in the pension system. His reforms won't solve the huge pension deficit, but the abolition of the *régimes spéciaux* is of great symbolic significance, for they are the most enduring sign of France's deeply hierarchical society.

Sarkozy even undermined the sacred cow of anti-Americanism and its concomitant Gaullist principle of French isolationism. By announcing, four decades after de Gaulle slammed the door, that France was returning to NATO's integrated command, Sarkozy not only broke another taboo, but also put an end to nearly two decades of hypocrisy. All through the nineties, French foreign policy required that any arrangement which put French forces at the disposal of a NATO operation had to be agreed in secret.* Sarkozy has simply decided to put an end to the myth of France's splendid isolation.

In December 2002 Laurent and I divorced. We had been married for fifteen years. When she found out that I was leaving her son, Madeleine came to have tea with me. She knew that I had met someone else and she was baffled by my decision to end the marriage, a move she saw as needlessly drastic.

'You change husbands,' she said. 'And you're only moving the furniture. Love comes and goes. In ten years' time you will see. You will reach the same point.'

Laurent fundamentally agreed with her, the pursuit of 'truth' being, in his eyes, vastly overrated and very selfish.

'Why can't you just have an *affair*, for God's sake?

---

* Daniel Vernet, *Le Monde*, 24 June 2008.

Why do you have to be such an Ayatollah of Truth?'

With Laurent, I had discovered France, had hated it, then loved it, hated it, then loved it again. What I didn't realise at the time was that with each discovery of some new, infuriating facet of her nature, as well as each new reconciliation, my resistance to this country was being worn down a little more. The constant struggle against my environment not only fashioned me, it fashioned my children. As they grew up, they bore witness to my frustration at each collision between the Anglo-Saxon Protestant value system of my upbringing and the Catholic cultural heritage of theirs.

'Stop knocking France,' they would say. 'England's worse. It's ugly and rainy and it smells of fried food and beer.'

Today the tables have turned. While I find myself, even without a French husband, becoming more and more deeply ensconced in French life, both my children are in the process of falling in love with my estranged motherland. I would never have guessed this development. Unlike my sister Irene's children, Jack and Ella were brought up French. They were educated in French schools and although I always spoke English to them, they would, until recently, generally answer me in French. My sister, like many English people who move to France, has never really cut the cord. She raised her children as English and they, unlike my children, both speak without the trace of a French accent.

I should have guessed, however, that reading Jack and

Ella Hilaire Belloc, Roald Dahl and Edward Lear instead of the Countess de Ségur or Jules Verne would probably set them on the path to abiding quirkiness. There is no nonsense or madness or indeed anything very dark about the stories that French parents tell their children. If the school psychiatrist had ever discovered the macabre and gruesome stories I would invent at my children's behest every night, she would have had the whole family in therapy in a flash. Laurent, under the influence of his mad English wife, invented a very good story about a homicidal *au pair* girl with a chainsaw who chased her charges through the woods every night after their parents had gone to sleep.

In spite of my decision to raise my children as French, it makes me happy to hear them discussing their new-found passion for all things English. Ella, who has recently returned from two months' work experience in London, is brimming with enthusiasm for the English sense of humour, as if she were the first to notice it.

'People aren't afraid to take the piss out of themselves in England. They don't care what other people think. There's none of that system we have in France where only one person in a group is allowed to be funny. You know – he or she's the clown and everyone else is the audience. In England everyone feels free to have a go.'

This, of course, is music to my ears.

'I love the fact that no one cares what they look like. And no one judges you. It's so . . . liberating!'

I remind myself that this was the girl who at sixteen

years old could not bear *not* to be looked at on the London Underground.

'I love the fact that when you go to a party in London you meet people from all countries and all backgrounds. In Paris, everyone stays in the gang they met at their *lycée* and they're all from exactly the same *milieu*. I met some French people who were going to the LSE and I had to get away. They only hang out with each other. It was completely suffocating.'

Now Ella says she would like to live and work in England for a while.

As for Jack, he too has made peace with his English roots. This is the survivor of the French national education system who decided that he wanted to be a philosopher. He had a brief stint doing work experience in London and came back wanting to be a filmmaker instead. He has taken a part-time job with a chain of English pubs in Paris while he finishes his Masters in philosophy. He tells me that he is amazed by the dedication of the British waiting staff and moved by their camaraderie.

'After a shift, we all sit down together and have a few beers, piss about. The French guys are sort of shut out. They don't get the jokes. They don't see the point of the work either. For them the job is just a means to an end and that affects everyone around them.'

So Jack discovers the Protestant work ethic and the notion of team spirit. This is the child who never ran a three-legged race or an egg-and-spoon race or saw his dad humiliate himself in a father's race. Brought up in a nation immune to the idea that it is the taking part that matters, Jack is slowly but surely discovering that winning is actually one of life's least interesting goals.

It is strange to me to watch my own children struggling, for the first time, with the very facets of their own culture that I found so infuriating when I first arrived twenty-three years ago. While they were growing up, I was blind to my own influence upon them. They seemed to me so wonderfully French that I would never have guessed that their Englishness would one day come and bite me on the bottom. Now that they're getting ready to leave for England, I find myself buried so deeply in this culture that I doubt I can ever escape it. France has swallowed me up, but not my children.

My relationship with France began with my relationship with Laurent. When the marriage ended, I assumed that my link to France would lessen in intensity. I was no longer speaking French all hours of the day, dreaming in French, arguing in French, loving in French. I thought I was no longer bound to this place. My children were grown up, so I could now choose: England or France. And then I discovered that I didn't want to leave. I know France now and in knowing her, I love her. Like the long-suffering spouse who realises, after all those years, that in spite of everything, there is no one in the world she would rather be with, I adore and despise this country in equal measure.

Bibliography

Aggoun, Lounis, and Jean-Baptiste Rivoire, *Françalgérie: Crimes et Mensonges d'Etats* (Editions La Découverte, 2004)

Auden, W. H., and Anne Fremantle, *The Protestant Mystics* (Weidenfeld & Nicolson, 1964)

Bergson, Henri, *Le Rire: Essai sur la Signification du Comique* (Alcan, 1900)

Bloch, Marc, *L'Etrange Défaite* (Poche, 1990)

Bonnet, Yves, *Nucléaire Iranien, Une Hypocrisie Internationale* (Michel Lafon, 2008)

Bourdrel, Philippe, *L'Epuration Sauvage 1944–1945* (Perrin, 2002)

Buchan, John, *Oliver Cromwell* (Hodder and Stoughton, 1934)

Colley, Linda, *Britons: Forging the Nation 1707–1837* (Yale University Press, 1992)

Debord, Guy, *La Société du Spectacle* (Buchet/Chastel, 1967)

Deloire, Christophe, and Christophe Dubois, *Sexus Politicus* (Albin Michel, 2006)

Freud, Sigmund, and William C. Bullitt, *Woodrow Wilson: A Psychological Study* (Weidenfeld & Nicolson, 1967)

d'Iribarne, Philippe, *L'Etrangeté Française* (Seuil, 2006)

Jung, Carl, *Aspects of the Feminine* (Princeton University Press, 1982)

Keniston McIntosh, Marjorie, *Working Women in English Society 1300–1620* (Cambridge University Press, 2005)

Michelet, Jules, *Notre France* (Lemerre, 1886)

Mitterrand, François, *L'Abeille et l'Architecte* (Flammarion, 1978)

Paxton, Robert, *La France de Vichy 1940–1944* (Seuil, 1973)

Bibliography

Peyrefitte, Alain, *Le Mal Français* (Plon, 1976)

Revel, Jean-François, *L'Obsession anti-Américaine* (Plon, 2002)

Rousso, Henry, *Le Syndrome de Vichy de 1944 à Nos Jours* (Seuil, 1987)

Sarkozy, Nicolas, *Témoignage* (XO Editions, 2006)

de Tocqueville, Alexis, *L'Ancien Régime et la Révolution* (Flammarion, 1998)

de Tocqueville, Alexis, *De la Démocratie en Amérique* (Flammarion, 1981)

Védrine, Hubert, *Les Mondes de François Mitterrand* (Fayard, 1996)

Weber, Max, *The Protestant Ethic and the Spirit of Capitalism*, trans. Peter Baehr and Gordon C. Wells (Penguin Books, 2002)

Index

Index

Index

Index